D1086650

Matthean and Lukan Special Material

Matthean and Lukan Special Material

A Brief Introduction with Texts in Greek and English

BRICE C. JONES

WIPF & STOCK · Eugene, Oregon

MATTHEAN AND LUKAN SPECIAL MATERIAL
A Brief Introduction with Texts in Greek and English

Copyright © 2011 Brice C. Jones. All rights reserved. Except for brief quotations in critical publications or reviews, no part of this book may be reproduced in any manner without prior written permission from the publisher. Write: Permissions, Wipf and Stock Publishers, 199 W. 8th Ave., Suite 3, Eugene, OR 97401.

Wipf & Stock
An Imprint of Wipf and Stock Publishers
199 W. 8th Ave., Suite 3
Eugene, OR 97401
www.wipfandstock.com

ISBN 13: 978-1-61097-737-1
Manufactured in the U.S.A.

Nestle-Aland, Novum Testamentum Graece, 27th Revised Edition, edited by Barbara Aland, Kurt Aland, Johannes Karavidopoulos, Carlo M. Martini, and Bruce M. Metzger in cooperation with the Institute for New Testament Textual Research, Münster/Westphalia, © 1993 Deutsche Bibelgesellschaft, Stuttgart. Used by permission.

[Scripture quotations are] from the New Revised Standard Version of the Bible, copyright © 1989 National Council of the Churches of Christ in the USA. Used by permission. All rights reserved.

Contents

Figures

Preface

FOR THE FIRST TIME, the Gospel material unique to both Matthew and Luke is brought together into one volume—in both Greek and English. For more than a century, New Testament scholars have asserted that Matthew and Luke drew on sources in addition to Q and Mark during the composition of their Gospels. For convenience, the non-paralleled material in Matthew has traditionally been labeled "M," and the non-paralleled material in Luke has traditionally been labeled "L." We learn only from Matthew, for example, particular stories like Joseph and Mary's escape to Egypt and the Great Commission; from Luke stories like the prodigal son and Jesus' appearance on the Emmaus road. Studying the material unique to each Gospel *in isolation* from their narrative contexts will allow students and scholars alike to engage these stories on their own. In this book, the individual special pericopae from Matthew and Luke are collected and arranged in Greek and English in the order in which they appear in the Greek New Testament. An introductory essay is provided to introduce readers to the Synoptic Problem, the notions of M and L and where they come from, what the parameters are for selection, and the critical debate, so that readers know how the selections were made and what is being asserted by their inclusion. This book will be a wonderful teaching tool for seminary and university professors, and will facilitate student engagement with distinctive Matthean and Lukan stories. It will also be a valuable resource for New Testament scholars doing research on this special material, since having it all in one place will no longer require them to search for the distinctive passages among the larger Gospel narratives. I hope readers will find this book a useful guide to Matthew and Luke's unique Gospel material.

Several people have helped to make this book possible. I wish to thank the editors of Wipf and Stock Publishers for accepting the present work for publication. I would especially like to thank my project editor, Christian Amondson, for helping me bring this work to publication

ix

by answering numerous questions throughout the writing and editorial stages. I am enormously grateful to several individuals who graciously read earlier drafts of my introductory essay (chapter 1), and offered many helpful comments and suggestions for improvement: Prof. Steve Walton (London School of Theology), Sonja Anderson (Yale University), and Myles Schoonover (Yale University). I am also indebted to Prof. Stanley E. Porter (McMaster Divinity College) for stimulating my thinking about the project in its early stages as well for offering helpful suggestions on how to approach the project. Finally, a special word of thanks goes to Dr. Paul Foster (University of Edinburgh), not only for reading chapter 1 and offering precious feedback, but also for being the model New Testament scholar and for giving a young, aspiring scholar his first opportunities to present and publish academic papers. For permission to reproduce copyright material, I am grateful to the Deutsche Bibelgesellshaft for the Greek text of the NA27, and to the National Council of Churches of Christ for the text of the *New Revised Standard Version* (NRSV).

Brice C. Jones
Montreal, Quebec

Abbreviations

ABD	Anchor Bible Dictionary
BETL	Bibliotheca Ephemeridum Theologicarum Lovaniensium
BiTS	Biblical Tools and Studies
ETL	*Ephemerides theologicae lovanienses*
ExpTim	*Expository Times*
JBL	*Journal of Biblical Literature*
JHC	*Journal of Higher Criticism*
JTS	*Journal of Theological Studies*
JSNTSup	Journal for the Study of the New Testament, Supplement Series
NGS	New Gospel Studies
NTS	*New Testament Studies*
SNTA	Studiorum Novi Testamenti Auxilia
SNTSMS	Society for New Testament Studies Monograph Series

1

Literary Relationships Among the Gospels

A Brief Introduction to the Synoptic Problem and Matthew and Luke's Special Source Material

INTRODUCTION

CRITICAL STUDY OF THE Gospels and their sources is a complex endeavor, not least because of the sundry developments over the last century and the lack of complete agreement among scholars today. There have been numerous attempts to work out the difficulties surrounding the Gospels and while there was a time when a consensus seemed to have been reached, that is not the case today. Current research on the Synoptic Gospels and the "Synoptic Problem" is thriving. Old theories continue to be re-evaluated and refined, and fresh studies are helping to stimulate scholarly research and move the discussion into new, exciting directions.[1]

The present book is meant to be a resource for the study of Matthew and Luke's sources and will, I hope, be a useful guide to those learning about the Synoptic Gospels generally and about the Synoptic Problem and Matthew and Luke's texts in particular. Since many will be coming to this subject for the first time, it will be helpful to provide a brief survey of the history of the Synoptic Problem before we move on to a discussion of Matthew and Luke's special source material and the purpose of this

---

1. Just recently a massive tome with a collection of individual essays on the Synoptic Problem was published, which is the result of an international conference on the Synoptic Problem that was held at Lincoln College, Oxford in April 2008. See Foster et al., *New Studies in the Synoptic Problem*.

book, since it is within this larger debate that the first and third Gospels' special material was brought to light.

THE SYNOPTIC PROBLEM

Today, the literary problem of understanding and explaining the literary relationships between the first three Gospels is known as the "Synoptic Problem."[2] Modern scholars have been dealing with this problem for many decades in an attempt to reconstruct the sources used in the composition of the Gospels. It should be noted, though, that modern biblical scholars are not to be credited with initially identifying the problems surrounding the Gospels and their sources. In the early church, some had begun to notice variations in the Gospels, such as, for example, Matthew's Sermon on the *Mount* and Luke's Sermon on the *Plain*. One of the earliest attempts to sort out these differences and inconsistencies was by Tatian (c. 125–185 CE), who produced a harmony of the four Gospels known as the *Diatessaron* ("through the four"), most likely in order to eliminate the discrepancies.[3] The early fourth century church father Eusebius mentions that Africanus (c. 160–240 CE) wrote a letter (*On the Supposed Discord between the Genealogies of Christ in Matthew and Luke*) to Aristides in which he established a harmony of the two, divergent accounts of the genealogy of Jesus in Matthew and Luke.[4] Augustine (354–430 CE) was the first person to make a serious effort to understand the literary relationships between the Gospels, and his approach was distinctly harmonistic. With respect to the order of the Gospels, he argued that Matthew was written first, then Mark, which used Matthew as a source, then Luke, which used both Mark and Matthew, and finally John, which used all three (the "Augustinian Hypothesis").[5] For centuries following Augustine, the critical debate experienced a hiatus, and the popular way to read the Gospels during this time was to conflate them, that is, to combine all the Gospel stories into one, big

---

2. Only a brief introduction will be given here. For a fuller treatment, see Stein, *The Synoptic Problem*; Nickle, *The Synoptic Gospels*; Kümmel, *Introduction to the New Testament*, 38–80.

3. It is not completely clear, however, what was Tatian's motivation for producing the *Diatessaron*. Eusebius claims that it was apparently to correct the apostles' style (*Hist. eccl.* 4.29).

4. *Hist. eccl.* 6.31.1.

5. *Cons.* I. 2.

"meta-Gospel" much like Tatian's *Diatessaron*. It was not until the eighteenth century that biblical scholars began to have a renewed interest in what Augustine and others had set out to do centuries prior, but this time the approach was much more critical and held to a higher level of scrutiny. During the Enlightenment (17th and 18th centuries), much of the work being done was centered on the life of Jesus and was driven by radical works that questioned the historical reliability of the Gospels, such as the "fragments" of Hermann Samuel Reimarus (1694–1768).[6] Reimarus had proposed that the Gospels, since they were composed deliberately by the disciples to warrant their own stances of power, are unreliable sources for understanding Jesus. While Reimarus' work was not well received among Christian scholars because of its radical assertions, it did force them into thinking objectively about the questions he raised and how to come up with possible solutions to the problems. In summary, this era experienced a development in Gospel research, and what began as a search for what can be known about the Jesus of history resulted in a critical examination of the primary sources that provided the information necessary for understanding him, namely, the Synoptic Gospels.

In 1776, J. J. Griesbach introduced and used the term "synoptic" (from σύνοψις, "seen together") to refer to the three Gospels that have so much material in common, namely, Matthew, Mark, and Luke. It had long been recognized that the Gospel of John was radically different from the other three Gospels, and so it was placed into a category of its own.[7] Griesbach challenged the Augustinian view of the order of the Gospels (i.e., Matthew, Mark, Luke) by proposing that Mark was the last Gospel to be written, itself being an abbreviation and conflation of Matthew and Luke (see figure 1).[8]

---

6. See Dawes, *The Historical Jesus Quest*, 54–86.

7. The *coup de grace* was administered in the early nineteenth century by D. F. Strauss (*The Life of Jesus*), who argued that John's presentation of Jesus was purely apologetic and dogmatic.

8. This theory was actually first proposed by Englishman Henry Owen in 1764 (*Observations on the Four Gospels*), but was popularized by and later attributed to Griesbach. See Williams, "The OWEN Hypothesis," 126–58.

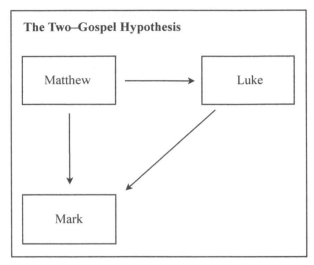

Figure 1

Today, the "Griesbach Hypothesis," more commonly referred to as the "Two-Gospel Hypothesis," is not held by the majority of New Testament scholars on account of several arguments that they claim make the hypothesis untenable. One of the main criticisms is the question of why Mark would have wanted to write his Gospel in the first place, since it is an abbreviation, and since almost all of his Gospel is preserved in fuller forms in Matthew and Luke. It is also suggested that Mark, had he abbreviated Matthew and Luke, would not have wanted to omit some of Jesus' most valued and well-known teachings. Despite these criticisms, some modern scholars have maintained the Two-Gospel Hypothesis, most notably William R. Farmer, whose work is largely responsible for the "revival" of the Two-Gospel hypothesis.[9]

Griesbach's hypothesis had a large following for several decades until a new hypothesis was put forward in the nineteenth century: Markan priority. A group of German and British scholars was responsible for leading the way, and it was not very long until Markan priority became the dominant view. This theory was designated the Two-Source (or Four-Source) or Oxford hypothesis,[10] and the most classic presenta-

9. Farmer, *The Synoptic Problem*. See also, *New Synoptic Studies*.

10. The phrase "Oxford Hypothesis" was used in reference to the various scholars of Oxford University in the early twentieth century who were instrumental in shaping the theory: J. Hawkins, W. Sanday, B. H. Streeter, W. C. Allen, J. Vernon Bartlet, W. E. Addis, N. P. Williams. A very important collection of individual essays written by these

tion of this perspective was B. H. Streeter's 1924 seminal work, *The Four Gospels*. The theory states that Mark was the first Gospel to be written, and that Matthew and Luke, writing independently of each other, used Mark as a source (see figure 2).

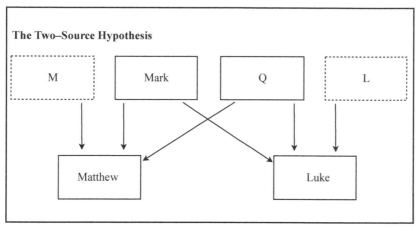

Figure 2

This would explain why there is so much material in common between the three Gospels (this material is referred to as the triple tradition). The theory also presupposes that Matthew and Luke used an additional source (non-extant today) made up of large portions of sayings material. This hypothetical source—hypothetical because it is lost to us today and must be reconstructed from the text of Matthew and Luke—was called Q, an abbreviation of *Quelle*, the German word for "source." The Sayings Source Q would help explain why there is so much material common to both Matthew and Luke (this material is referred to as the double tradition), but absent from Mark. These are the basic principles of the Two-Source hypothesis. B. H. Streeter went on to propose two, additional sources—a source that accounted for the material unique to Matthew (which he called "M"), and a source that accounted for the material unique to Luke (which he called "L"). Streeter modified the basic Two-Source hypothesis to formulate the *Four*-Source hypothesis in order to account for these additional sources (more on which below), and he produced five fundamental reasons for accepting the priority of Mark:

scholars on the Synoptic Problem was published in 1911 (Sanday, *Studies in the Synoptic Problem By Members of the University of Oxford*).

1. Matthew reproduces 90 percent of Mark, and Luke more than 50 percent.

2. The majority of *actual words* of Mark are reproduced by Matthew and Luke.

3. Matthew and Luke generally agree with Mark's order: where Matthew deserts Mark's order, Luke supports it, and vice versa.

4. Matthew and Luke tone down Mark's offensive language and improve his literary style.

5. The way in which Matthew and Luke distribute Markan and non-Markan material suggests that both had a written copy of Mark and had to determine precisely how to combine this material with other material.

These five points came to be seen as the standard arguments for Markan priority, and, while the details continue to be debated, they are still considered by most to be compelling arguments in the case for Markan priority.

The Two-Source hypothesis was so well received that it went largely unchallenged for decades. The majority of scholars in the twentieth century accepted the theory emphatically, and some were so persuaded by the solution that they no longer thought of it as a hypothesis, but a rule. But beginning in the middle of the twentieth century, a few scholars began to call the Two-Source hypothesis into question. One of the first major critiques was that of B. C. Butler in 1951, who argued for Matthean priority and demonstrated that the phenomenon of order merely situates Mark in a middle, not prior, position (known as the "Lachmann Fallacy").[11] He suggested that Luke used Matthew and Mark as a source, but that Mark's only source was "proto-Matthew," an Aramaic document. Shortly thereafter, A. M. Farrer wrote an essay titled, "On Dispensing with Q," in which he argued that Markan priority should be maintained, but without assuming the existence of a Q source.[12] His main theory was that Mark was written first, that Matthew used Mark, and that Luke was dependent on Matthew and Mark. If accepted, this theory would explain why Matthew and Luke had so much material in common: because Luke used Matthew. Thus, Q could be jettisoned. Today, the "Farrer theory" is

11. Butler, *The Originality of St. Matthew.*
12. Farrer, "On Dispensing with Q," 55–88.

a minority position, but it has found support among some scholars, such as Michael Goulder[13] and Mark Goodacre;[14] the theory is often referred to as the "Farrer-Goulder" or "Farrer-Goulder-Goodacre hypothesis."

There are several arguments against the Two-Source hypothesis, but I will here mention only three major ones. The first is the so-called "Mark-Q overlaps," which refer to the stories that existed in both Mark and Q. Where these pericopae overlap, Matthew and Luke chose to include both the Markan and Q versions. For example, the saying on divorce in Mark 10:11–12 is also found in Q 16:18 (Matt 5:32//Luke 16:18).[15] Most advocates of the Two-Source hypothesis, however, do not think that the Mark-Q overlaps pose any real threat, since two independent yet similar traditions are bound to have existed prior to the composition of the Gospels as we know them.

Another argument against the Two-Source hypothesis is the so-called "minor agreements," which refer to the few cases where Matthew and Luke agree on wording with each other against Mark. This poses a problem for the view that Matthew and Luke both used Mark, but did not use each other as a source. A common example is the phrase, "Who is it that struck you?" in the scene of the interrogation of Jesus in Matt 26:68 and Luke 22:64. Matthew and Luke both contain the phrase, but Mark lacks it. How is this to be explained if Matthew and Luke did not know each other and the story is not found in Q? One way is to say that Matthew and Luke knew of an *oral* Markan tradition that was in some places slightly different than what they had in their *written* copies of Mark. Another way to explain it is that, somewhere along the way, the Gospel texts were corrupted, and the minor agreements between Matthew and Luke were removed from Mark, or, alternatively, were added to Matthew and Luke. More likely perhaps is the view that the minor agreements between Matthew and Luke against Mark arose due to harmonization in the early history of the text. While the minor agreements do pose difficulties to the Two-Source hypothesis, the number of significant minor agreements is small, and the explanations for their ex-

---

13. See Goulder, "Is Q a Juggernaut?," 667–81.

14. See Goodacre, *The Synoptic Problem*.

15. I have followed the standard way of referring to Q passages: by their Lukan chapter and verses. So, Q 16:18 is the Q saying found in Luke 16:18 and Matt 5:32.

istence are compelling enough to maintain the Two-Source hypothesis with confidence.[16]

Another difficulty is that the theory requires a hypothetical document, which is not physically attested outside of the Gospels. This position is especially popular among advocates of solutions to the Synoptic Problem that posit Matthean and Lukan dependence. There are difficulties in sustaining this argument, however, and most scholars tend to believe that the Two-Source hypothesis makes the most sense of the data.[17] Despite these and other attempts to overthrow the Two-Source hypothesis, it still stands as the dominant position within New Testament scholarship today, although it is not the rule as was once thought in the first half of the twentieth century. Research on the Synoptic Problem will continue, and numerous books and articles will keep the printing presses churning for quite some time. The merits of the Two-Source hypothesis have been shown, but refinements to the theory will doubtless still need to be made, and further thinking will of course be stimulated as a result of the questions raised from other sides of the debate.[18]

MATTHEW AND LUKE'S SPECIAL MATERIAL: "M" AND "L"

Since the context of the debate about Gospel sources has been established, we are now ready to move on to a more detailed discussion of Matthew and Luke's source material. As mentioned above, Streeter was the first to postulate the idea that Matthew and Luke used two special sources of their own in addition to Mark and Q. For convenience, he

---

16. The definition of terms in the study of minor agreements is a matter of scholarly debate. One question is how to quantitatively account for the minor agreements. For example, is the six-word phrase "Who is it that struck you?" one minor agreement or six? For a detailed discussion of these issues, see Boring, "The 'Minor Agreements,'" 227–251.

17. For an excellent discussion and defense of the Sayings Source Q by one of the most influential Q scholars, see Kloppenborg, Q, The Earliest Gospel. See also, ibid., Excavating Q; ibid., The Shape of Q.

18. In 1969, E.P. Sanders wrote an important work on the Gospels (The Tendencies of the Synoptic Tradition) at the end of which he states, "I rather suspect that when and if a new view of the Synoptic problem becomes accepted, it will be more flexible and complicated than the tidy two-document hypothesis. With all due respect for scientific preference for the simpler view, the evidence seems to require a more complicated one" (279).

called these "M" and "L." He contended that the provenance and dates of these four sources could be discerned:[19]

1. M, Matthew's special source, was composed in Jerusalem in approximately 60 CE.

2. L, Luke's special source, was composed in Caesarea in approximately 60 CE.

3. Q is a Greek document that was composed in Antioch in approximately 50 CE.

4. Mark was written in Rome in 66 CE.

Prior to Streeter, it had been thought that the material unique to Matthew and Luke was simply due to the fact that each Gospel writer utilized two recensions of Q: Q^{Mt} and Q^{Lk}. Streeter was critical of this view, claiming that "it conceals the unconscious assumption that they [Matthew and Luke] used no other documents, or, at least, none of anything like the same value as the 'Big Two.'"[20] In his view, it was not necessary to extend the boundaries of Q merely so that all of the extra material in Matthew and Luke could be assigned to it. The simplest explanation, according to Streeter, is that Matthew and Luke each had at their disposal a special written source on which they drew during the composition of their respective Gospels, that Matthew did not know Luke's special source, and Luke did not know Matthew's. Stories such as the Laborers in the Vineyard, the Pearl of Great Price, and the Great Commission are peculiar to Matthew, while stories such as the Good Samaritan, the Prodigal Son, and the Pharisee and the Publican are all unique to Luke. As a result of Streeter's source analysis, all Gospel material could be placed into neat source categories. Furthermore, the parameters of Q could now be confined only to the material that is shared between Matthew and Luke, eliminating the need to force material into Q that did not seem to fit.

Streeter also argued that Luke assembled Q and L together into one composite document, which Streeter called "Proto-Luke," and later produced a larger work (the Gospel of Luke as we know it) by incorporating portions of Mark and prefixing an infancy narrative. This composite document (Q + L) was, according to Streeter, Luke's preferred source, and this would explain why Luke omits so much more of Mark's contents

19. See the chart in Streeter, *Four Gospels*, 150.
20. Ibid., 227.

than Matthew does (especially the "great omission," Mark 6:45—8:26), as well as why Luke contains a considerable amount of additional stories, which are especially prevalent in his "Travel Narrative" (9:51—19:44). Matthew is said to have combined Mark, Q, M, and what Streeter called the "Antiochene Tradition," into what is now known as the Gospel of Matthew. Streeter argued that M had a "Judaistic tendency," by which he means a "later Judaistic reaction against the Petro-Pauline liberalism in the matter of the Gentile Mission and the observance of the Law."[21]

STATUS QUAESTIONIS

The basic premise of Streeter's argument—that Matthew and Luke used special sources in addition to Q and Mark—is fairly widely accepted today, although many of its details have been disputed, especially the theory of Proto-Luke.[22] Many questions remain, however, as to the real nature of M and L, and certain methodological constraints on the reconstruction of the content of M and L exist. Because Streeter's Four-Source theory was a precursor of redaction criticism, his analysis failed to give the evangelists' editorial work the kind of attention it deserves. Modern New Testament scholarship is in a much better position to address issues vis-à-vis the evangelists' attempts to rework their sources, and this certainly has consequences for the theory of M and L. For example, were M and L written sources, as Streeter suggested, or were they oral sources, or a combination of both? Were these stories indeed found in sources available to Matthew and Luke, or did they compose them? If M and L consist of a combination of written and oral sources, how then do we distinguish one from the other? Similarly, if M and L are composed of a combination of pre-Gospel tradition and free composition, then how do we distinguish between them? Still, most scholars remain wary of any attempt to place Matthew and Luke's special material into tightly defined categories since we have no manuscript evidence to support any conclusion. Moreover, any reconstruction of an original M or L source remains highly speculative. But, the same could theoretically be said about Q, for

21. Ibid., 512. See also the excellent article on the M source by Foster, "The M Source," 591–616.

22. For a critique of the Proto-Luke hypothesis, see Gilmour, "A Critical Re-Examination of Proto-Luke," 143–52.

which no manuscript exists, and yet there have been many attempts to reconstruct Q's original wording.[23]

Indeed, some scholars doubt the existence of an M or L source altogether. Udo Schnelle, for example, has argued that there is no such thing as an L source, since "there are linguistic differences within the special materials, and the whole bears the marks of Luke's own editorial work."[24] Schnelle's remark concerning the editorial work of Luke underscores the greatest difficulty in determining the special material of M and L: it is hard to know what is editorial and what is pre-Gospel source material.

But, others (and perhaps most) are accepting of the existence of M and L in some form; the main issue is whether they are to be understood as written or oral sources. There are two important works that are often cited in support of M and L. The first is by Stephenson Brooks, titled, *Matthew's Community: The Evidence of His Special Sayings Material*. In this work, Brooks applies three criteria to determine whether or not certain sayings unique to Matthew were a product of his own redaction: style, vocabulary, and content. Passages that fail to pass the test of these criteria are labeled M material. Brooks finds three strands of tradition and uses them ultimately to locate three groups within the one Matthean community: 1) Christian Jews who belong to a non-Christian synagogue; 2) non-Jewish Christians; 3) Christians in conflict with Israel. M, and the sundry ideologies standing behind it, is said to have a theological orientation that is consonant with that of the author of Matthew. Brooks claims that it is unlikely that M was a unified written source, although some portions of it may have been written. Rather, M existed predominantly, and possibly entirely, in oral form, and came to Matthew in various ways. Unfortunately, Brooks's analysis, which was limited to the sayings material, succeeds primarily in proving that some of the sayings in Matthew's special source were ideologically diverse. His attempt to locate specific Matthean groups behind certain sayings is not entirely convincing, especially if we take seriously the view that each of the Gospels may not have been written for a specific church or group

23. The most notable attempt at reconstructing Q was that of the International Q Project (IQP), which consisted of more than forty scholars from North America and Europe and resulted in a massive volume on the outcome of the project. See Robinson, et al., *The Critical Edition of Q*. For an abbreviated version of the IQP's reconstruction of Q, as well as a nice Q synopsis, see the very useful handbook by Neirynck, *Q-Parallels*. See also the fine work by Fleddermann, *Q: A Reconstruction and Commentary*.

24. Schnelle, *The History and Theology of the New Testament Writings*, 250.

of churches (e.g., the Matthean community, Markan community, Lukan community, Johannine community).[25] It is always difficult to say with any real certainty what was the historical setting behind a piece of tradition, and so Brooks's heavy form-critical approach is dubious.

The second work is Kim Paffenroth's monograph titled, *The Story of Jesus according to L.* Focusing on the unparalleled material in Luke, Paffenroth, unlike Brooks whose sole focus was the sayings material, gives attention to the entire gamut of special material in Luke and spends all of chapter 2 "limiting the material to be considered" (the chapter's title). Paffenroth argues that an L source did exist and can be distinguished from Lukan composition and redaction: "The L material does seem to have enough dissimilarities from Lukan style, form, and content to make it probable that this material is pre-Lukan."[26] If material can be explained as having its origin in 1) a Lukan redaction of Mark, 2) the Sayings Source Q, or 3) Luke's free composition, then it is eliminated from the list of L material. Paffenroth claims that the material he assigns to L is from a unified, and most probably written, source that was composed by Jewish-Christians in Palestine sometime between 40 and 60 CE.[27] His book ends with his own reconstruction of L material, which is based on the analysis he sets out in chapter two (see the Appendix in this book).

These two works demonstrate well the difficulties involved in any attempt to isolate strands of pre-existing Gospel traditions that make up the hypothetical sources M and L. Both Brooks and Paffenroth made careful and painstaking efforts to show whether a certain saying or story might stem from a previous tradition, or whether it was in fact a product of Matthew or Luke's own editorial activity. And this is no easy matter, especially if we consider that Matthew and Luke may not have redacted their sources in a consistent manner. For example, if Streeter is right that Luke preferred his special source over Mark, then it may be the case that he devoted more time to editing it. In any case, what is becoming increasingly clear is that the unparalleled material in Matthew and

25. For a challenge against the common assumption that Gospels were written for specific communities, see the important article by Richard Bauckham, "For Whom Were Gospels Written?" See also idem., *Jesus and the Eyewitnesses.*

26. Paffenroth, *The Story of Jesus according to L,* 143.

27. Here, Paffenroth is in agreement with Streeter on the provenance and characteristic of M, though he allows for an earlier date than Streeter.

Luke is not as coherent as Streeter had initially thought, and that it is instead more likely to have consisted of a variety of sources that came to the evangelists in diverse ways. Given this possibility that M and L were not unified sources, it is also unclear as to whether or not a theological profile can be established for M and L. The future of the debate over Matthew and Luke's special sources is uncertain, but it will require more attention than is currently being given to it in order to move the discussion forward. Still, introductions to the New Testament and the Gospels, as well as commentaries, will for the most part assume these sources, and they will continue to inform readers that Matthew and Luke probably used them.

PURPOSE AND METHOD OF BOOK

The idea for this book developed during my own studies of the Gospels as a graduate student. I would often sit in my Greek exegesis classes on the Gospels with my Q parallels and Synopsis,[28] and wish that I had at my disposal a small book that printed the special material of Matthew and Luke. Moreover, it is difficult enough to find a list of what is generally thought to constitute M and L material.[29] The student is often required to peruse the plethora of commentaries on the Gospels and introductions to the New Testament in order to find such a list, only to discover that most of them do not include a list of this kind. It is certainly possible (and perhaps even more advantageous) for the student to cull from the pages of the Greek New Testament all the unparalleled Matthean and Lukan material, but this would take a great deal of time. So this book is largely meant to serve a practical purpose: to bring all the material unique to Matthew and Luke into one place so that it can be studied on its own, in isolation from the larger Gospel narratives. There is currently a useful book like this for the hypothetical Sayings Source Q: a synopsis in which the Greek text of Matthew is printed on the left page, and the Greek text of Luke on the right page.[30]

A few things should be said about the method of the selection process and what is being asserted by the inclusion of the material. First, the

28. Aland, *Synopsis Quattuor Evangeliorum.*

29. To much surprise, even Streeter fails to list the contents of M and L in his classic work, *The Four Gospels.*

30. Neirynck, *Q-Parallels.* An English equivalent of this Q synopsis may be found in Borg, *The Lost Gospel Q.*

contents of chapters 2 and 3 do not represent a *reconstruction* of M and L. I am not using any criteria to delimit material in the ways that Brooks and Paffenroth have done, and the reader should not think of the contents as the definitive M source or L source. Rather, I am simply selecting material that is unique to Matthew and Luke that might possibly have originated from M and L.

THE FOLLOWING IS A LIST OF UNIQUE MATTHEAN MATERIAL:[31]

Genealogy of Jesus	1:2–17
Birth of Jesus	1:18–25
Visit of the Magi	2:1–12
Flight to Egypt	2:13–21
Fulfillment of the Law	5:17–20
Concerning Anger	5:21–24
Concerning Adultery	5:27–29
Concerning Divorce	5:31
Concerning Oaths	5:33–37
An Eye for an Eye	5:38–39a
Love for Enemies	5:43
Concerning Piety	6:1–19
Pearls Before Swine	7:6
Coming Persecutions	10:21–23
Call to Rest	11:28–30
Parables (Weeds, Pearl, Net, Treasure)	13:24–30, 36–52
Peter Walks on Water	14:28–31
Jesus Blesses Peter	16:17–19
Jesus and the Temple Tax	17:24–27
Reproving One Who Sins	18:15–20
Peter's Question about Forgiveness	18:21–22
Parable of Unforgiving Servant	18:23–35
Parable of Laborers in the Vineyard	20:1–16
Parable of Two Sons	21:28–32
Prohibition of Titles	23:2–5, 7–12
Jesus Denounces the Scribes and Pharisees	23:15–22
Parable of the Ten Bridesmaids	25:1–13

31. This list and the one that follows are modified versions of the ones found in Powell, *Fortress Introduction to The Gospels*, 62 and 86–87, respectively.

Sheep and the Goats	25:31–46
Death of Judas	27:3–10
Pilate Washes His Hands	27:24–25
Resurrection of Saints	27:52–53
Guard at the Tomb	27:62–66
Report of the Guard	28:11–15
Great Commission	28:16–20

THE FOLLOWING IS A LIST OF UNIQUE LUKAN MATERIAL:

Prologue	1:1–4
Birth of John Foretold	1:5–25
Birth of Jesus Foretold	1:26–38
Mary Visits Elizabeth	1:39–56
Birth of John the Baptist	1:57–80
Birth of Jesus	2:1–20
Jesus is Presented in the Temple	2:21–38
The Boy Jesus in the Temple	2:41–52
John Replies to Questions	3:10–14
Genealogy of Jesus	3:23–38
Good News to the Poor	4:14–23, 25–30
Call of First Disciples/Catch of Fish	5:1–11
Jesus Raises Widow's Son at Nain	7:11–17
Jesus Anointed by a Sinful Woman	7:36–50
Women Accompany Jesus	8:1–3
Samaritan Village Rejects Jesus	9:51–56
Return of the Seventy	10:17–20
Parable of the Good Samaritan	10:29–37
Jesus Visits Martha and Mary	10:38–42
Parable of Friend at Midnight	11:5–8
Parable of the Rich Fool	12:13–21
Repent or Perish	13:1–5
Parable of the Barren Fig Tree	13:6–9
Jesus Heals a Crippled Woman	13:10–17
Jesus Heals Man with Dropsy	14:1–6
Humility and Hospitality	14:7–14
Cost of Discipleship	14:28–33
Parable of Lost Coin	15:8–10
Parable of Prodigal Son	15:11–32

Parable of Dishonest Manager	16:1–12
Parable of Rich Man and Lazarus	16:19–31
Jesus Cleanses Ten Lepers	17:11–19
Parable of Widow and Unjust Judge	18:1–8
Parable of Pharisee and Tax Collector	18:9–14
Jesus and Zacchaeus	19:1–10
Jesus Weeps over Jerusalem	19:41–44
Jesus' Prayer for Peter	22:31–32
Purse, Bag, and Sword	22:35–38
Jesus Before Herod	23:6–12
Pilate Declares Jesus Innocent	23:13–16
Sayings about Jesus' Death	23:28–31, 34, 43, 46
Road to Emmaus	24:13–35
Appearance to the Disciples	24:36–49
Jesus' Ascension	24:50–53

Second, my inclusion of these particular passages is not meant to suggest that some of the material cannot possibly be assigned to Q, the redaction of the evangelists, or some other source. For example, I am assigning Luke's preface (1:1–4) and infancy narrative (1:5—2:52) to the special material of Luke, simply because these are stories that are unique to Luke. Yet most would argue that these stories derive from Luke himself and were possibly incorporated by him at a later date,[32] while others contend that there was a distinctive "Baptist source" behind Luke 1.[33] The point is that not all of the passages incorporated here are conclusive; they represent only what is broadly considered *possible* M and L material.[34] Third, although the Matthean and Lukan special material is printed here, I am not advocating that these were written sources. As I have already mentioned, there is considerable debate about whether Matthew and Luke's special material was oral or written or a combination of both, and this is a question that remains unanswered. Finally, as I have intimated above, my aim is not to make the final decisions on what should or should not be counted as authentic M or L material.

32. So Paffenroth, *The Story of Jesus according to L*, 28.

33. For a discussion of the "Baptist source," see Wink, *John the Baptist in the Gospel Tradition*, 60–72.

34. Cf. the contents of the lists above to those in Goodacre, *The Synoptic Problem*, 43 and 45–46, respectively.

There must, however, be a starting point from which investigations into the true nature of M and L source material can begin, and the selections herein are representative of the stories that can be used as a basis for further testing and analysis. In summary, I am collating material that is unique to either Matthew or Luke (the so-called *Sondergut* traditions) and presenting these singly attested synoptic traditions in a format that is readily accessible. Such material could derive from special source material available only to either Matthew or Luke, it could be the redactional creation of either evangelist, or it could be Q material that only one of the evangelists has chosen to reproduce. However, here it will be left to readers to determine which of these explanations best accounts for the singly attested tradition under consideration.

My greatest hope is that this book can be used as a teaching tool to help advanced students of the Gospels learn the stories and sayings unique to Matthew and Luke. It is ideal for use in the classroom in which the Gospels as well as Greek exegesis courses are being taught and studied. As such, this book serves as an introduction as well as a work manual. It may also prove to be a useful resource for New Testament scholars whose research is centered on the sources behind Matthew and Luke. One potential advantage of having all of Matthew and Luke's unique material separated into individual units is that, by reading one story to the next without the interruption of Markan or Q material, certain literary aspects of M or L, such as important themes or narrative devices and so forth, may become more apparent. In this respect, the utility of the book lies in its ability to provide a clearer image of the stories that tend to get mixed in with other stories in Matthew and Luke.

The above indices of M and L material will be employed in this book, and its individual contents will be printed in both Greek and English. The Greek text is from the *Novum Testamentum Graece* by Nestle-Aland, currently in its twenty-seventh edition (NA27), and the English translation is from the New Revised Standard Version (NRSV). The bibliography includes works that I have consulted in writing this introductory chapter and compiling the M and L material, as well as other books and articles for further reading.

2

Greek–English Texts
of Matthew's Unique Material

GENEALOGY OF JESUS (1:2–17)

Greek

² Ἀβραὰμ ἐγέννησεν τὸν Ἰσαάκ, Ἰσαὰκ δὲ ἐγέννησεν τὸν Ἰακώβ, Ἰακὼβ δὲ
ἐγέννησεν τὸν Ἰούδαν καὶ τοὺς ἀδελφοὺς αὐτοῦ, ³ Ἰούδας δὲ ἐγέννησεν τὸν
Φάρες καὶ τὸν Ζάρα ἐκ τῆς Θαμάρ, Φάρες δὲ ἐγέννησεν τὸν Ἐσρώμ, Ἐσρὼμ
δὲ ἐγέννησεν τὸν Ἀράμ, ⁴ Ἀρὰμ δὲ ἐγέννησεν τὸν Ἀμιναδάβ, Ἀμιναδὰβ δὲ
ἐγέννησεν τὸν Ναασσών, Ναασσὼν δὲ ἐγέννησεν τὸν Σαλμών, ⁵ Σαλμὼν
δὲ ἐγέννησεν τὸν Βόες ἐκ τῆς Ῥαχάβ, Βόες δὲ ἐγέννησεν τὸν Ἰωβὴδ ἐκ τῆς
Ῥούθ, Ἰωβὴδ δὲ ἐγέννησεν τὸν Ἰεσσαί, ⁶ Ἰεσσαὶ δὲ ἐγέννησεν τὸν Δαυὶδ
τὸν βασιλέα. Δαυὶδ δὲ ἐγέννησεν τὸν Σολομῶνα ἐκ τῆς τοῦ Οὐρίου, ⁷
Σολομὼν δὲ ἐγέννησεν τὸν Ῥοβοάμ, Ῥοβοὰμ δὲ ἐγέννησεν τὸν Ἀβιά, Ἀβιὰ
δὲ ἐγέννησεν τὸν Ἀσάφ, ⁸ Ἀσὰφ δὲ ἐγέννησεν τὸν Ἰωσαφάτ, Ἰωσαφὰτ δὲ
ἐγέννησεν τὸν Ἰωράμ, Ἰωρὰμ δὲ ἐγέννησεν τὸν Ὀζίαν, ⁹ Ὀζίας δὲ ἐγέννησεν
τὸν Ἰωαθάμ, Ἰωαθὰμ δὲ ἐγέννησεν τὸν Ἀχάζ, Ἀχὰζ δὲ ἐγέννησεν τὸν
Ἐζεκίαν, ¹⁰ Ἐζεκίας δὲ ἐγέννησεν τὸν Μανασσῆ, Μανασσῆς δὲ ἐγέννησεν τὸν
Ἀμώς, Ἀμὼς δὲ ἐγέννησεν τὸν Ἰωσίαν, ¹¹ Ἰωσίας δὲ ἐγέννησεν τὸν Ἰεχονίαν
καὶ τοὺς ἀδελφοὺς αὐτοῦ ἐπὶ τῆς μετοικεσίας Βαβυλῶνος. ¹² Μετὰ δὲ τὴν
μετοικεσίαν Βαβυλῶνος Ἰεχονίας ἐγέννησεν τὸν Σαλαθιήλ, Σαλαθιὴλ δὲ
ἐγέννησεν τὸν Ζοροβαβέλ, ¹³ Ζοροβαβὲλ δὲ ἐγέννησεν τὸν Ἀβιούδ, Ἀβιοὺδ
δὲ ἐγέννησεν τὸν Ἐλιακίμ, Ἐλιακὶμ δὲ ἐγέννησεν τὸν Ἀζώρ, ¹⁴ Ἀζὼρ δὲ
ἐγέννησεν τὸν Σαδώκ, Σαδὼκ δὲ ἐγέννησεν τὸν Ἀχίμ, Ἀχὶμ δὲ ἐγέννησεν
τὸν Ἐλιούδ, ¹⁵ Ἐλιοὺδ δὲ ἐγέννησεν τὸν Ἐλεάζαρ, Ἐλεάζαρ δὲ ἐγέννησεν
τὸν Ματθάν, Ματθὰν δὲ ἐγέννησεν τὸν Ἰακώβ, ¹⁶ Ἰακὼβ δὲ ἐγέννησεν τὸν

Ἰωσὴφ τὸν ἄνδρα Μαρίας, ἐξ ἧς ἐγεννήθη Ἰησοῦς ὁ λεγόμενος Χριστός. ¹⁷
Πᾶσαι οὖν αἱ γενεαὶ ἀπὸ Ἀβραὰμ ἕως Δαυὶδ γενεαὶ δεκατέσσαρες, καὶ ἀπὸ
Δαυὶδ ἕως τῆς μετοικεσίας Βαβυλῶνος γενεαὶ δεκατέσσαρες, καὶ ἀπὸ τῆς
μετοικεσίας Βαβυλῶνος ἕως τοῦ Χριστοῦ γενεαὶ δεκατέσσαρες.

English

² Abraham was the father of Isaac, and Isaac the father of Jacob, and
Jacob the father of Judah and his brothers, ³ and Judah the father of Perez
and Zerah by Tamar, and Perez the father of Hezron, and Hezron the
father of Aram, ⁴ and Aram the father of Aminadab, and Aminadab the
father of Nahshon, and Nahshon the father of Salmon, ⁵ and Salmon the
father of Boaz by Rahab, and Boaz the father of Obed by Ruth, and Obed
the father of Jesse, ⁶ and Jesse the father of King David. And David was
the father of Solomon by the wife of Uriah, ⁷ and Solomon the father of
Rehoboam, and Rehoboam the father of Abijah, and Abijah the father
of Asaph, ⁸ and Asaph the father of Jehoshaphat, and Jehoshaphat the
father of Joram, and Joram the father of Uzziah, ⁹ and Uzziah the father of Jotham, and Jotham the father of Ahaz, and Ahaz the father of
Hezekiah, ¹⁰ and Hezekiah the father of Manasseh, and Manasseh the
father of Amos, and Amos the father of Josiah, ¹¹ and Josiah the father
of Jechoniah and his brothers, at the time of the deportation to Babylon.
¹² And after the deportation to Babylon: Jechoniah was the father of
Salathiel, and Salathiel the father of Zerubbabel, ¹³ and Zerubbabel the
father of Abiud, and Abiud the father of Eliakim, and Eliakim the father
of Azor, ¹⁴ and Azor the father of Zadok, and Zadok the father of Achim,
and Achim the father of Eliud, ¹⁵ and Eliud the father of Eleazar, and
Eleazar the father of Matthan, and Matthan the father of Jacob, ¹⁶ and
Jacob the father of Joseph the husband of Mary, of whom Jesus was born,
who is called the Messiah. ¹⁷ So all the generations from Abraham to
David are fourteen generations; and from David to the deportation to
Babylon, fourteen generations; and from the deportation to Babylon to
the Messiah, fourteen generations.

BIRTH OF JESUS (1:18–25)

Greek

¹⁸ Τοῦ δὲ Ἰησοῦ Χριστοῦ ἡ γένεσις οὕτως ἦν. μνηστευθείσης τῆς μητρὸς αὐτοῦ Μαρίας τῷ Ἰωσήφ, πρὶν ἢ συνελθεῖν αὐτοὺς εὑρέθη ἐν γαστρὶ ἔχουσα ἐκ πνεύματος ἁγίου. ¹⁹ Ἰωσὴφ δὲ ὁ ἀνὴρ αὐτῆς, δίκαιος ὢν καὶ μὴ θέλων αὐτὴν δειγματίσαι, ἐβουλήθη λάθρᾳ ἀπολῦσαι αὐτήν. ²⁰ ταῦτα δὲ αὐτοῦ ἐνθυμηθέντος ἰδοὺ ἄγγελος κυρίου κατ' ὄναρ ἐφάνη αὐτῷ λέγων, Ἰωσὴφ υἱὸς Δαυίδ, μὴ φοβηθῇς παραλαβεῖν Μαριὰμ τὴν γυναῖκά σου, τὸ γὰρ ἐν αὐτῇ γεννηθὲν ἐκ πνεύματός ἐστιν ἁγίου· ²¹ τέξεται δὲ υἱὸν καὶ καλέσεις τὸ ὄνομα αὐτοῦ Ἰησοῦν, αὐτὸς γὰρ σώσει τὸν λαὸν αὐτοῦ ἀπὸ τῶν ἁμαρτιῶν αὐτῶν. ²² Τοῦτο δὲ ὅλον γέγονεν ἵνα πληρωθῇ τὸ ῥηθὲν ὑπὸ κυρίου διὰ τοῦ προφήτου λέγοντος, ²³ Ἰδοὺ ἡ παρθένος ἐν γαστρὶ ἕξει καὶ τέξεται υἱόν, καὶ καλέσουσιν τὸ ὄνομα αὐτοῦ Ἐμμανουήλ, ὅ ἐστιν μεθερμηνευόμενον Μεθ' ἡμῶν ὁ θεός. ²⁴ ἐγερθεὶς δὲ [ὁ] Ἰωσὴφ ἀπὸ τοῦ ὕπνου ἐποίησεν ὡς προσέταξεν αὐτῷ ὁ ἄγγελος κυρίου καὶ παρέλαβεν τὴν γυναῖκα αὐτοῦ· ²⁵ καὶ οὐκ ἐγίνωσκεν αὐτὴν ἕως οὗ ἔτεκεν υἱόν· καὶ ἐκάλεσεν τὸ ὄνομα αὐτοῦ Ἰησοῦν.

English

¹⁸ Now the birth of Jesus the Messiah took place in this way. When his mother Mary had been engaged to Joseph, but before they lived together, she was found to be with child from the Holy Spirit. ¹⁹ Her husband Joseph, being a righteous man and unwilling to expose her to public disgrace, planned to dismiss her quietly. ²⁰ But just when he had resolved to do this, an angel of the Lord appeared to him in a dream and said, "Joseph, son of David, do not be afraid to take Mary as your wife, for the child conceived in her is from the Holy Spirit. ²¹ She will bear a son, and you are to name him Jesus, for he will save his people from their sins." ²² All this took place to fulfill what had been spoken by the Lord through the prophet: ²³ "Look, the virgin shall conceive and bear a son, and they shall name him Emmanuel," which means, "God is with us." ²⁴ When Joseph awoke from sleep, he did as the angel of the Lord commanded him; he took her as his wife, ²⁵ but had no marital relations with her until she had borne a son; and he named him Jesus.

VISIT OF THE MAGI (2:1-12)

Greek

¹ Τοῦ δὲ Ἰησοῦ γεννηθέντος ἐν Βηθλέεμ τῆς Ἰουδαίας ἐν ἡμέραις Ἡρῴδου τοῦ βασιλέως, ἰδοὺ μάγοι ἀπὸ ἀνατολῶν παρεγένοντο εἰς Ἱεροσόλυμα ² λέγοντες, Ποῦ ἐστιν ὁ τεχθεὶς βασιλεὺς τῶν Ἰουδαίων; εἴδομεν γὰρ αὐτοῦ τὸν ἀστέρα ἐν τῇ ἀνατολῇ καὶ ἤλθομεν προσκυνῆσαι αὐτῷ. ³ ἀκούσας δὲ ὁ βασιλεὺς Ἡρῴδης ἐταράχθη καὶ πᾶσα Ἱεροσόλυμα μετ' αὐτοῦ, ⁴ καὶ συναγαγὼν πάντας τοὺς ἀρχιερεῖς καὶ γραμματεῖς τοῦ λαοῦ ἐπυνθάνετο παρ' αὐτῶν ποῦ ὁ Χριστὸς γεννᾶται. ⁵ οἱ δὲ εἶπαν αὐτῷ, Ἐν Βηθλέεμ τῆς Ἰουδαίας· οὕτως γὰρ γέγραπται διὰ τοῦ προφήτου· ⁶ Καὶ σύ, Βηθλέεμ γῆ Ἰούδα, οὐδαμῶς ἐλαχίστη εἶ ἐν τοῖς ἡγεμόσιν Ἰούδα· ἐκ σοῦ γὰρ ἐξελεύσεται ἡγούμενος, ὅστις ποιμανεῖ τὸν λαόν μου τὸν Ἰσραήλ. ⁷ Τότε Ἡρῴδης λάθρα καλέσας τοὺς μάγους ἠκρίβωσεν παρ' αὐτῶν τὸν χρόνον τοῦ φαινομένου ἀστέρος, ⁸ καὶ πέμψας αὐτοὺς εἰς Βηθλέεμ εἶπεν, Πορευθέντες ἐξετάσατε ἀκριβῶς περὶ τοῦ παιδίου· ἐπὰν δὲ εὕρητε ἀπαγγείλατέ μοι, ὅπως κἀγὼ ἐλθὼν προσκυνήσω αὐτῷ. ⁹ οἱ δὲ ἀκούσαντες τοῦ βασιλέως ἐπορεύθησαν, καὶ ἰδοὺ ὁ ἀστὴρ ὃν εἶδον ἐν τῇ ἀνατολῇ προῆγεν αὐτοὺς ἕως ἐλθὼν ἐστάθη ἐπάνω οὗ ἦν τὸ παιδίον. ¹⁰ ἰδόντες δὲ τὸν ἀστέρα ἐχάρησαν χαρὰν μεγάλην σφόδρα. ¹¹ καὶ ἐλθόντες εἰς τὴν οἰκίαν εἶδον τὸ παιδίον μετὰ Μαρίας τῆς μητρὸς αὐτοῦ, καὶ πεσόντες προσεκύνησαν αὐτῷ, καὶ ἀνοίξαντες τοὺς θησαυροὺς αὐτῶν προσήνεγκαν αὐτῷ δῶρα, χρυσὸν καὶ λίβανον καὶ σμύρναν. ¹² καὶ χρηματισθέντες κατ' ὄναρ μὴ ἀνακάμψαι πρὸς Ἡρῴδην, δι' ἄλλης ὁδοῦ ἀνεχώρησαν εἰς τὴν χώραν αὐτῶν.

English

¹ In the time of King Herod, after Jesus was born in Bethlehem of Judea, wise men from the East came to Jerusalem, ² asking, "Where is the child who has been born king of the Jews? For we observed his star at its rising, and have come to pay him homage." ³ When King Herod heard this, he was frightened, and all Jerusalem with him; ⁴ and calling together all the chief priests and scribes of the people, he inquired of them where the Messiah was to be born. ⁵ They told him, "In Bethlehem of Judea; for so it has been written by the prophet: ⁶ 'And you, Bethlehem, in the land of Judah, are by no means least among the rulers of Judah; for from you shall come a ruler who is to shepherd my people Israel.'" ⁷ Then Herod secretly called for the wise men and learned from them the exact time

when the star had appeared. [8] Then he sent them to Bethlehem, saying, "Go and search diligently for the child; and when you have found him, bring me word so that I may also go and pay him homage." [9] When they had heard the king, they set out; and there, ahead of them, went the star that they had seen at its rising, until it stopped over the place where the child was. [10] When they saw that the star had stopped, they were overwhelmed with joy. [11] On entering the house, they saw the child with Mary his mother; and they knelt down and paid him homage. Then, opening their treasure-chests, they offered him gifts of gold, frankincense, and myrrh. [12] And having been warned in a dream not to return to Herod, they left for their own country by another road.

FLIGHT TO EGYPT (2:13–21)

Greek

[13] Ἀναχωρησάντων δὲ αὐτῶν ἰδοὺ ἄγγελος κυρίου φαίνεται κατ' ὄναρ τῷ Ἰωσὴφ λέγων, Ἐγερθεὶς παράλαβε τὸ παιδίον καὶ τὴν μητέρα αὐτοῦ καὶ φεῦγε εἰς Αἴγυπτον, καὶ ἴσθι ἐκεῖ ἕως ἂν εἴπω σοι· μέλλει γὰρ Ἡρῴδης ζητεῖν τὸ παιδίον τοῦ ἀπολέσαι αὐτό. [14] ὁ δὲ ἐγερθεὶς παρέλαβεν τὸ παιδίον καὶ τὴν μητέρα αὐτοῦ νυκτὸς καὶ ἀνεχώρησεν εἰς Αἴγυπτον, [15] καὶ ἦν ἐκεῖ ἕως τῆς τελευτῆς Ἡρῴδου· ἵνα πληρωθῇ τὸ ῥηθὲν ὑπὸ κυρίου διὰ τοῦ προφήτου λέγοντος, Ἐξ Αἰγύπτου ἐκάλεσα τὸν υἱόν μου. [16] Τότε Ἡρῴδης ἰδὼν ὅτι ἐνεπαίχθη ὑπὸ τῶν μάγων ἐθυμώθη λίαν, καὶ ἀποστείλας ἀνεῖλεν πάντας τοὺς παῖδας τοὺς ἐν Βηθλέεμ καὶ ἐν πᾶσι τοῖς ὁρίοις αὐτῆς ἀπὸ διετοῦς καὶ κατωτέρω, κατὰ τὸν χρόνον ὃν ἠκρίβωσεν παρὰ τῶν μάγων. [17] τότε ἐπληρώθη τὸ ῥηθὲν διὰ Ἰερεμίου τοῦ προφήτου λέγοντος, [18] Φωνὴ ἐν Ῥαμὰ ἠκούσθη, κλαυθμὸς καὶ ὀδυρμὸς πολύς· Ῥαχὴλ κλαίουσα τὰ τέκνα αὐτῆς, καὶ οὐκ ἤθελεν παρακληθῆναι, ὅτι οὐκ εἰσίν. [19] Τελευτήσαντος δὲ τοῦ Ἡρῴδου ἰδοὺ ἄγγελος κυρίου φαίνεται κατ' ὄναρ τῷ Ἰωσὴφ ἐν Αἰγύπτῳ [20] λέγων, Ἐγερθεὶς παράλαβε τὸ παιδίον καὶ τὴν μητέρα αὐτοῦ καὶ πορεύου εἰς γῆν Ἰσραήλ, τεθνήκασιν γὰρ οἱ ζητοῦντες τὴν ψυχὴν τοῦ παιδίου. [21] ὁ δὲ ἐγερθεὶς παρέλαβεν τὸ παιδίον καὶ τὴν μητέρα αὐτοῦ καὶ εἰσῆλθεν εἰς γῆν Ἰσραήλ.

English

[13] Now after they had left, an angel of the Lord appeared to Joseph in a dream and said, "Get up, take the child and his mother, and flee to

Egypt, and remain there until I tell you; for Herod is about to search for the child, to destroy him." [14] Then Joseph got up, took the child and his mother by night, and went to Egypt, [15] and remained there until the death of Herod. This was to fulfill what had been spoken by the Lord through the prophet, "Out of Egypt I have called my son."

[16] When Herod saw that he had been tricked by the wise men, he was infuriated, and he sent and killed all the children in and around Bethlehem who were two years old or under, according to the time that he had learned from the wise men. [17] Then was fulfilled what had been spoken through the prophet Jeremiah: [18] "A voice was heard in Ramah, wailing and loud lamentation, Rachel weeping for her children; she refused to be consoled, because they are no more." [19] When Herod died, an angel of the Lord suddenly appeared in a dream to Joseph in Egypt and said, [20] "Get up, take the child and his mother, and go to the land of Israel, for those who were seeking the child's life are dead." [21] Then Joseph got up, took the child and his mother, and went to the land of Israel.

FULFILLMENT OF THE LAW (5:17–20)

Greek

[17] Μὴ νομίσητε ὅτι ἦλθον καταλῦσαι τὸν νόμον ἢ τοὺς προφήτας· οὐκ ἦλθον καταλῦσαι ἀλλὰ πληρῶσαι. [18] ἀμὴν γὰρ λέγω ὑμῖν, ἕως ἂν παρέλθῃ ὁ οὐρανὸς καὶ ἡ γῆ, ἰῶτα ἓν ἢ μία κεραία οὐ μὴ παρέλθῃ ἀπὸ τοῦ νόμου ἕως ἂν πάντα γένηται. [19] ὃς ἐὰν οὖν λύσῃ μίαν τῶν ἐντολῶν τούτων τῶν ἐλαχίστων καὶ διδάξῃ οὕτως τοὺς ἀνθρώπους, ἐλάχιστος κληθήσεται ἐν τῇ βασιλείᾳ τῶν οὐρανῶν· ὃς δ’ ἂν ποιήσῃ καὶ διδάξῃ, οὗτος μέγας κληθήσεται ἐν τῇ βασιλείᾳ τῶν οὐρανῶν. [20] λέγω γὰρ ὑμῖν ὅτι ἐὰν μὴ περισσεύσῃ ὑμῶν ἡ δικαιοσύνη πλεῖον τῶν γραμματέων καὶ Φαρισαίων, οὐ μὴ εἰσέλθητε εἰς τὴν βασιλείαν τῶν οὐρανῶν.

English

[17] "Do not think that I have come to abolish the law or the prophets; I have come not to abolish but to fulfill. [18] For truly I tell you, until heaven and earth pass away, not one letter, not one stroke of a letter, will pass from the law until all is accomplished. [19] Therefore, whoever breaks one of the least of these commandments, and teaches others to do the same,

will be called least in the kingdom of heaven; but whoever does them and teaches them will be called great in the kingdom of heaven. [20] For I tell you, unless your righteousness exceeds that of the scribes and Pharisees, you will never enter the kingdom of heaven."

CONCERNING ANGER (5:21–24)

Greek

[21] Ἠκούσατε ὅτι ἐρρέθη τοῖς ἀρχαίοις, Οὐ φονεύσεις· ὃς δ᾽ ἂν φονεύσῃ, ἔνοχος ἔσται τῇ κρίσει. [22] ἐγὼ δὲ λέγω ὑμῖν ὅτι πᾶς ὁ ὀργιζόμενος τῷ ἀδελφῷ αὐτοῦ ἔνοχος ἔσται τῇ κρίσει· ὃς δ᾽ ἂν εἴπῃ τῷ ἀδελφῷ αὐτοῦ, Ῥακά, ἔνοχος ἔσται τῷ συνεδρίῳ· ὃς δ᾽ ἂν εἴπῃ, Μωρέ, ἔνοχος ἔσται εἰς τὴν γέενναν τοῦ πυρός. [23] ἐὰν οὖν προσφέρῃς τὸ δῶρόν σου ἐπὶ τὸ θυσιαστήριον κἀκεῖ μνησθῇς ὅτι ὁ ἀδελφός σου ἔχει τι κατὰ σοῦ, [24] ἄφες ἐκεῖ τὸ δῶρόν σου ἔμπροσθεν τοῦ θυσιαστηρίου, καὶ ὕπαγε πρῶτον διαλλάγηθι τῷ ἀδελφῷ σου, καὶ τότε ἐλθὼν πρόσφερε τὸ δῶρόν σου.

English

[21]"You have heard that it was said to those of ancient times, 'You shall not murder'; and 'whoever murders shall be liable to judgment.' [22] But I say to you that if you are angry with a brother or sister, you will be liable to judgment; and if you insult a brother or sister, you will be liable to the council; and if you say, 'You fool,' you will be liable to the hell of fire. [23] So when you are offering your gift at the altar, if you remember that your brother or sister has something against you, [24] leave your gift there before the altar and go; first be reconciled to your brother or sister, and then come and offer your gift."

CONCERNING ADULTERY (5:27–29)

Greek

[27] Ἠκούσατε ὅτι ἐρρέθη, Οὐ μοιχεύσεις. [28] ἐγὼ δὲ λέγω ὑμῖν ὅτι πᾶς ὁ βλέπων γυναῖκα πρὸς τὸ ἐπιθυμῆσαι αὐτὴν ἤδη ἐμοίχευσεν αὐτὴν ἐν τῇ καρδίᾳ αὐτοῦ. [29] εἰ δὲ ὁ ὀφθαλμός σου ὁ δεξιὸς σκανδαλίζει σε, ἔξελε αὐτὸν καὶ βάλε ἀπὸ σοῦ· συμφέρει γάρ σοι ἵνα ἀπόληται ἓν τῶν μελῶν σου καὶ μὴ ὅλον τὸ σῶμά σου βληθῇ εἰς γέενναν.

English

²⁷ "You have heard that it was said, 'You shall not commit adultery.' ²⁸ But I say to you that everyone who looks at a woman with lust has already committed adultery with her in his heart. ²⁹ If your right eye causes you to sin, tear it out and throw it away; it is better for you to lose one of your members than for your whole body to be thrown into hell."

CONCERNING DIVORCE (5:31)

Greek

³¹ Ἐρρέθη δέ, Ὃς ἂν ἀπολύσῃ τὴν γυναῖκα αὐτοῦ, δότω αὐτῇ ἀποστάσιον.

English

³¹ "It was also said, 'Whoever divorces his wife, let him give her a certificate of divorce.'"

CONCERNING OATHS (5:33–37)

Greek

³³ Πάλιν ἠκούσατε ὅτι ἐρρέθη τοῖς ἀρχαίοις, Οὐκ ἐπιορκήσεις, ἀποδώσεις δὲ τῷ κυρίῳ τοὺς ὅρκους σου. ³⁴ ἐγὼ δὲ λέγω ὑμῖν μὴ ὀμόσαι ὅλως· μήτε ἐν τῷ οὐρανῷ, ὅτι θρόνος ἐστὶν τοῦ θεοῦ· ³⁵ μήτε ἐν τῇ γῇ, ὅτι ὑποπόδιόν ἐστιν τῶν ποδῶν αὐτοῦ· μήτε εἰς Ἱεροσόλυμα, ὅτι πόλις ἐστὶν τοῦ μεγάλου βασιλέως· ³⁶ μήτε ἐν τῇ κεφαλῇ σου ὀμόσῃς, ὅτι οὐ δύνασαι μίαν τρίχα λευκὴν ποιῆσαι ἢ μέλαιναν. ³⁷ ἔστω δὲ ὁ λόγος ὑμῶν ναὶ ναί, οὒ οὔ· τὸ δὲ περισσὸν τούτων ἐκ τοῦ πονηροῦ ἐστιν.

English

³³ "Again, you have heard that it was said to those of ancient times, 'You shall not swear falsely, but carry out the vows you have made to the Lord.' ³⁴ But I say to you, Do not swear at all, either by heaven, for it is the throne of God, ³⁵ or by the earth, for it is his footstool, or by Jerusalem, for it is the city of the great King. ³⁶ And do not swear by your head, for you cannot make one hair white or black. ³⁷ Let your word be 'Yes, Yes' or 'No, No'; anything more than this comes from the evil one."

AN EYE FOR AN EYE (5:38-39A)

Greek

[38] Ἠκούσατε ὅτι ἐρρέθη, Ὀφθαλμὸν ἀντὶ ὀφθαλμοῦ καὶ ὀδόντα ἀντὶ ὀδόντος. [39A] ἐγὼ δὲ λέγω ὑμῖν μὴ ἀντιστῆναι τῷ πονηρῷ·

English

[38] "You have heard that it was said, 'An eye for an eye and a tooth for a tooth.' [39A] But I say to you, do not resist an evildoer."

LOVE FOR ENEMIES (5:43)

Greek

[43] Ἠκούσατε ὅτι ἐρρέθη, Ἀγαπήσεις τὸν πλησίον σου καὶ μισήσεις τὸν ἐχθρόν σου.

English

[43] "You have heard that it was said, 'You shall love your neighbor and hate your enemy.'"

CONCERNING PIETY (6:1-19)

Greek

[1] Προσέχετε [δὲ] τὴν δικαιοσύνην ὑμῶν μὴ ποιεῖν ἔμπροσθεν τῶν ἀνθρώπων πρὸς τὸ θεαθῆναι αὐτοῖς· εἰ δὲ μήγε, μισθὸν οὐκ ἔχετε παρὰ τῷ πατρὶ ὑμῶν τῷ ἐν τοῖς οὐρανοῖς. [2] Ὅταν οὖν ποιῇς ἐλεημοσύνην, μὴ σαλπίσῃς ἔμπροσθέν σου, ὥσπερ οἱ ὑποκριταὶ ποιοῦσιν ἐν ταῖς συναγωγαῖς καὶ ἐν ταῖς ῥύμαις, ὅπως δοξασθῶσιν ὑπὸ τῶν ἀνθρώπων· ἀμὴν λέγω ὑμῖν, ἀπέχουσιν τὸν μισθὸν αὐτῶν. [3] σοῦ δὲ ποιοῦντος ἐλεημοσύνην μὴ γνώτω ἡ ἀριστερά σου τί ποιεῖ ἡ δεξιά σου, [4] ὅπως ᾖ σου ἡ ἐλεημοσύνη ἐν τῷ κρυπτῷ· καὶ ὁ πατήρ σου ὁ βλέπων ἐν τῷ κρυπτῷ [αὐτὸς] ἀποδώσει σοι. [5] Καὶ ὅταν προσεύχησθε, οὐκ ἔσεσθε ὡς οἱ ὑποκριταί· ὅτι φιλοῦσιν ἐν ταῖς συναγωγαῖς καὶ ἐν ταῖς γωνίαις τῶν πλατειῶν ἑστῶτες προσεύχεσθαι, ὅπως φανῶσιν τοῖς ἀνθρώποις· ἀμὴν λέγω ὑμῖν, ἀπέχουσιν τὸν μισθὸν αὐτῶν. [6]

σὺ δὲ ὅταν προσεύχῃ, εἴσελθε εἰς τὸ ταμεῖόν σου καὶ κλείσας τὴν θύραν σου
πρόσευξαι τῷ πατρί σου τῷ ἐν τῷ κρυπτῷ· καὶ ὁ πατήρ σου ὁ βλέπων ἐν
τῷ κρυπτῷ ἀποδώσει σοι. ⁷ Προσευχόμενοι δὲ μὴ βατταλογήσητε ὥσπερ
οἱ ἐθνικοί, δοκοῦσιν γὰρ ὅτι ἐν τῇ πολυλογίᾳ αὐτῶν εἰσακουσθήσονται. ⁸
μὴ οὖν ὁμοιωθῆτε αὐτοῖς, οἶδεν γὰρ ὁ πατὴρ ὑμῶν ὧν χρείαν ἔχετε πρὸ τοῦ
ὑμᾶς αἰτῆσαι αὐτόν. ⁹ Οὕτως οὖν προσεύχεσθε ὑμεῖς· Πάτερ ἡμῶν ὁ ἐν τοῖς
οὐρανοῖς, ἁγιασθήτω τὸ ὄνομά σου, ¹⁰ ἐλθέτω ἡ βασιλεία σου, γενηθήτω τὸ
θέλημά σου, ὡς ἐν οὐρανῷ καὶ ἐπὶ γῆς. ¹¹ Τὸν ἄρτον ἡμῶν τὸν ἐπιούσιον δὸς
ἡμῖν σήμερον· ¹² καὶ ἄφες ἡμῖν τὰ ὀφειλήματα ἡμῶν, ὡς καὶ ἡμεῖς ἀφήκαμεν
τοῖς ὀφειλέταις ἡμῶν· ¹³ καὶ μὴ εἰσενέγκῃς ἡμᾶς εἰς πειρασμόν, ἀλλὰ ῥῦσαι
ἡμᾶς ἀπὸ τοῦ πονηροῦ. ¹⁴ Ἐὰν γὰρ ἀφῆτε τοῖς ἀνθρώποις τὰ παραπτώματα
αὐτῶν, ἀφήσει καὶ ὑμῖν ὁ πατὴρ ὑμῶν ὁ οὐράνιος· ¹⁵ ἐὰν δὲ μὴ ἀφῆτε τοῖς
ἀνθρώποις, οὐδὲ ὁ πατὴρ ὑμῶν ἀφήσει τὰ παραπτώματα ὑμῶν. ¹⁶ Ὅταν
δὲ νηστεύητε, μὴ γίνεσθε ὡς οἱ ὑποκριταὶ σκυθρωποί, ἀφανίζουσιν γὰρ τὰ
πρόσωπα αὐτῶν ὅπως φανῶσιν τοῖς ἀνθρώποις νηστεύοντες· ἀμὴν λέγω
ὑμῖν, ἀπέχουσιν τὸν μισθὸν αὐτῶν. ¹⁷ σὺ δὲ νηστεύων ἄλειψαί σου τὴν
κεφαλὴν καὶ τὸ πρόσωπόν σου νίψαι, ¹⁸ ὅπως μὴ φανῇς τοῖς ἀνθρώποις
νηστεύων ἀλλὰ τῷ πατρί σου τῷ ἐν τῷ κρυφαίῳ· καὶ ὁ πατήρ σου ὁ βλέπων
ἐν τῷ κρυφαίῳ ἀποδώσει σοι. ¹⁹ Μὴ θησαυρίζετε ὑμῖν θησαυροὺς ἐπὶ τῆς
γῆς, ὅπου σὴς καὶ βρῶσις ἀφανίζει, καὶ ὅπου κλέπται διορύσσουσιν καὶ
κλέπτουσιν·

English

¹ "Beware of practicing your piety before others in order to be seen by
them; for then you have no reward from your Father in heaven. ² "So
whenever you give alms, do not sound a trumpet before you, as the
hypocrites do in the synagogues and in the streets, so that they may be
praised by others. Truly I tell you, they have received their reward. ³ But
when you give alms, do not let your left hand know what your right hand
is doing, ⁴ so that your alms may be done in secret; and your Father who
sees in secret will reward you. ⁵ "And whenever you pray, do not be like
the hypocrites; for they love to stand and pray in the synagogues and at
the street corners, so that they may be seen by others. Truly I tell you,
they have received their reward. ⁶ But whenever you pray, go into your
room and shut the door and pray to your Father who is in secret; and
your Father who sees in secret will reward you. ⁷ "When you are praying,
do not heap up empty phrases as the Gentiles do; for they think that they
will be heard because of their many words. ⁸ Do not be like them, for

your Father knows what you need before you ask him. ⁹ "Pray then in this way: Our Father in heaven, hallowed be your name. ¹⁰ Your kingdom come. Your will be done, on earth as it is in heaven. ¹¹ Give us this day our daily bread. ¹² And forgive us our debts, as we also have forgiven our debtors. ¹³ And do not bring us to the time of trial, but rescue us from the evil one. ¹⁴ For if you forgive others their trespasses, your heavenly Father will also forgive you; ¹⁵ but if you do not forgive others, neither will your Father forgive your trespasses. ¹⁶ "And whenever you fast, do not look dismal, like the hypocrites, for they disfigure their faces so as to show others that they are fasting. Truly I tell you, they have received their reward. ¹⁷ But when you fast, put oil on your head and wash your face, ¹⁸ so that your fasting may be seen not by others but by your Father who is in secret; and your Father who sees in secret will reward you. ¹⁹ "Do not store up for yourselves treasures on earth, where moth and rust consume and where thieves break in and steal."

PEARLS BEFORE SWINE (7:6)

Greek

⁶ Μὴ δῶτε τὸ ἅγιον τοῖς κυσίν, μηδὲ βάλητε τοὺς μαργαρίτας ὑμῶν ἔμπροσθεν τῶν χοίρων, μήποτε καταπατήσουσιν αὐτοὺς ἐν τοῖς ποσὶν αὐτῶν καὶ στραφέντες ῥήξωσιν ὑμᾶς.

English

⁶ "Do not give what is holy to dogs; and do not throw your pearls before swine, or they will trample them under foot and turn and maul you."

COMING PERSECUTIONS (10:21–23)

Greek

²¹ παραδώσει δὲ ἀδελφὸς ἀδελφὸν εἰς θάνατον καὶ πατὴρ τέκνον, καὶ ἐπαναστήσονται τέκνα ἐπὶ γονεῖς καὶ θανατώσουσιν αὐτούς. ²² καὶ ἔσεσθε μισούμενοι ὑπὸ πάντων διὰ τὸ ὄνομά μου· ὁ δὲ ὑπομείνας εἰς τέλος οὗτος σωθήσεται. ²³ ὅταν δὲ διώκωσιν ὑμᾶς ἐν τῇ πόλει ταύτῃ, φεύγετε εἰς τὴν ἑτέραν· ἀμὴν γὰρ λέγω ὑμῖν, οὐ μὴ τελέσητε τὰς πόλεις τοῦ Ἰσραὴλ ἕως [ἂν] ἔλθῃ ὁ υἱὸς τοῦ ἀνθρώπου.

English

²¹ "Brother will betray brother to death, and a father his child, and children will rise against parents and have them put to death; ²² and you will be hated by all because of my name. But the one who endures to the end will be saved. ²³ When they persecute you in one town, flee to the next; for truly I tell you, you will not have gone through all the towns of Israel before the Son of Man comes."

CALL TO REST (11:28–30)

Greek

²⁸ Δεῦτε πρός με πάντες οἱ κοπιῶντες καὶ πεφορτισμένοι, κἀγὼ ἀναπαύσω ὑμᾶς. ²⁹ ἄρατε τὸν ζυγόν μου ἐφ᾽ ὑμᾶς καὶ μάθετε ἀπ᾽ ἐμοῦ, ὅτι πραΰς εἰμι καὶ ταπεινὸς τῇ καρδίᾳ, καὶ εὑρήσετε ἀνάπαυσιν ταῖς ψυχαῖς ὑμῶν· ³⁰ ὁ γὰρ ζυγός μου χρηστὸς καὶ τὸ φορτίον μου ἐλαφρόν ἐστιν.

English

²⁸ "Come to me, all you that are weary and are carrying heavy burdens, and I will give you rest. ²⁹ Take my yoke upon you, and learn from me; for I am gentle and humble in heart, and you will find rest for your souls. ³⁰ For my yoke is easy, and my burden is light."

PARABLES (WEEDS, PEARL, NET, TREASURE) (13:24–30, 36–52)

Greek

²⁴ Ἄλλην παραβολὴν παρέθηκεν αὐτοῖς λέγων, Ὡμοιώθη ἡ βασιλεία τῶν οὐρανῶν ἀνθρώπῳ σπείραντι καλὸν σπέρμα ἐν τῷ ἀγρῷ αὐτοῦ. ²⁵ ἐν δὲ τῷ καθεύδειν τοὺς ἀνθρώπους ἦλθεν αὐτοῦ ὁ ἐχθρὸς καὶ ἐπέσπειρεν ζιζάνια ἀνὰ μέσον τοῦ σίτου καὶ ἀπῆλθεν. ²⁶ ὅτε δὲ ἐβλάστησεν ὁ χόρτος καὶ καρπὸν ἐποίησεν, τότε ἐφάνη καὶ τὰ ζιζάνια. ²⁷ προσελθόντες δὲ οἱ δοῦλοι τοῦ οἰκοδεσπότου εἶπον αὐτῷ, Κύριε, οὐχὶ καλὸν σπέρμα ἔσπειρας ἐν τῷ σῷ ἀγρῷ; πόθεν οὖν ἔχει ζιζάνια; ²⁸ ὁ δὲ ἔφη αὐτοῖς, Ἐχθρὸς ἄνθρωπος τοῦτο ἐποίησεν. οἱ δὲ δοῦλοι λέγουσιν αὐτῷ, Θέλεις οὖν ἀπελθόντες συλλέξωμεν αὐτά; ²⁹ ὁ δέ φησιν, Οὔ, μήποτε συλλέγοντες τὰ ζιζάνια ἐκριζώσητε ἅμα αὐτοῖς τὸν σῖτον. ³⁰ ἄφετε συναυξάνεσθαι ἀμφότερα ἕως τοῦ θερισμοῦ·

καὶ ἐν καιρῷ τοῦ θερισμοῦ ἐρῶ τοῖς θερισταῖς, Συλλέξατε πρῶτον τὰ ζιζάνια καὶ δήσατε αὐτὰ εἰς δέσμας πρὸς τὸ κατακαῦσαι αὐτά, τὸν δὲ σῖτον συναγάγετε εἰς τὴν ἀποθήκην μου.

³⁶ Τότε ἀφεὶς τοὺς ὄχλους ἦλθεν εἰς τὴν οἰκίαν. καὶ προσῆλθον αὐτῷ οἱ μαθηταὶ αὐτοῦ λέγοντες, Διασάφησον ἡμῖν τὴν παραβολὴν τῶν ζιζανίων τοῦ ἀγροῦ. 37 ὁ δὲ ἀποκριθεὶς εἶπεν, Ὁ σπείρων τὸ καλὸν σπέρμα ἐστὶν ὁ υἱὸς τοῦ ἀνθρώπου· ³⁸ ὁ δὲ ἀγρός ἐστιν ὁ κόσμος· τὸ δὲ καλὸν σπέρμα, οὗτοί εἰσιν οἱ υἱοὶ τῆς βασιλείας· τὰ δὲ ζιζάνιά εἰσιν οἱ υἱοὶ τοῦ πονηροῦ, ³⁹ ὁ δὲ ἐχθρὸς ὁ σπείρας αὐτά ἐστιν ὁ διάβολος· ὁ δὲ θερισμὸς συντέλεια αἰῶνός ἐστιν, οἱ δὲ θερισταὶ ἄγγελοί εἰσιν. ⁴⁰ ὥσπερ οὖν συλλέγεται τὰ ζιζάνια καὶ πυρὶ καίεται, οὕτως ἔσται ἐν τῇ συντελείᾳ τοῦ αἰῶνος· ⁴¹ ἀποστελεῖ ὁ υἱὸς τοῦ ἀνθρώπου τοὺς ἀγγέλους αὐτοῦ, καὶ συλλέξουσιν ἐκ τῆς βασιλείας αὐτοῦ πάντα τὰ σκάνδαλα καὶ τοὺς ποιοῦντας τὴν ἀνομίαν, ⁴² καὶ βαλοῦσιν αὐτοὺς εἰς τὴν κάμινον τοῦ πυρός· ἐκεῖ ἔσται ὁ κλαυθμὸς καὶ ὁ βρυγμὸς τῶν ὀδόντων. ⁴³ Τότε οἱ δίκαιοι ἐκλάμψουσιν ὡς ὁ ἥλιος ἐν τῇ βασιλείᾳ τοῦ πατρὸς αὐτῶν. ὁ ἔχων ὦτα ἀκουέτω. ⁴⁴ Ὁμοία ἐστὶν ἡ βασιλεία τῶν οὐρανῶν θησαυρῷ κεκρυμμένῳ ἐν τῷ ἀγρῷ, ὃν εὑρὼν ἄνθρωπος ἔκρυψεν, καὶ ἀπὸ τῆς χαρᾶς αὐτοῦ ὑπάγει καὶ πωλεῖ πάντα ὅσα ἔχει καὶ ἀγοράζει τὸν ἀγρὸν ἐκεῖνον. ⁴⁵ Πάλιν ὁμοία ἐστὶν ἡ βασιλεία τῶν οὐρανῶν ἀνθρώπῳ ἐμπόρῳ ζητοῦντι καλοὺς μαργαρίτας· ⁴⁶ εὑρὼν δὲ ἕνα πολύτιμον μαργαρίτην ἀπελθὼν πέπρακεν πάντα ὅσα εἶχεν καὶ ἠγόρασεν αὐτόν. ⁴⁷ Πάλιν ὁμοία ἐστὶν ἡ βασιλεία τῶν οὐρανῶν σαγήνῃ βληθείσῃ εἰς τὴν θάλασσαν καὶ ἐκ παντὸς γένους συναγαγούσῃ· ⁴⁸ ἣν ὅτε ἐπληρώθη ἀναβιβάσαντες ἐπὶ τὸν αἰγιαλὸν καὶ καθίσαντες συνέλεξαν τὰ καλὰ εἰς ἄγγη, τὰ δὲ σαπρὰ ἔξω ἔβαλον. ⁴⁹ οὕτως ἔσται ἐν τῇ συντελείᾳ τοῦ αἰῶνος· ἐξελεύσονται οἱ ἄγγελοι καὶ ἀφοριοῦσιν τοὺς πονηροὺς ἐκ μέσου τῶν δικαίων ⁵⁰ καὶ βαλοῦσιν αὐτοὺς εἰς τὴν κάμινον τοῦ πυρός· ἐκεῖ ἔσται ὁ κλαυθμὸς καὶ ὁ βρυγμὸς τῶν ὀδόντων. ⁵¹ Συνήκατε ταῦτα πάντα; λέγουσιν αὐτῷ, Ναί. ⁵² ὁ δὲ εἶπεν αὐτοῖς, Διὰ τοῦτο πᾶς γραμματεὺς μαθητευθεὶς τῇ βασιλείᾳ τῶν οὐρανῶν ὅμοιός ἐστιν ἀνθρώπῳ οἰκοδεσπότῃ ὅστις ἐκβάλλει ἐκ τοῦ θησαυροῦ αὐτοῦ καινὰ καὶ παλαιά.

English

²⁴ He put before them another parable: "The kingdom of heaven may be compared to someone who sowed good seed in his field; ²⁵ but while everybody was asleep, an enemy came and sowed weeds among the wheat, and then went away. ²⁶ So when the plants came up and bore

grain, then the weeds appeared as well. ²⁷ And the slaves of the house-holder came and said to him, 'Master, did you not sow good seed in your field? Where, then, did these weeds come from?' ²⁸ He answered, 'An enemy has done this.' The slaves said to him, 'Then do you want us to go and gather them?' ²⁹ But he replied, 'No; for in gathering the weeds you would uproot the wheat along with them. ³⁰ Let both of them grow to-gether until the harvest; and at harvest time I will tell the reapers, Collect the weeds first and bind them in bundles to be burned, but gather the wheat into my barn.'"

³⁶ Then he left the crowds and went into the house. And his dis-ciples approached him, saying, "Explain to us the parable of the weeds of the field." ³⁷ He answered, "The one who sows the good seed is the Son of Man; ³⁸ the field is the world, and the good seed are the children of the kingdom; the weeds are the children of the evil one, ³⁹ and the enemy who sowed them is the devil; the harvest is the end of the age, and the reapers are angels. ⁴⁰ Just as the weeds are collected and burned up with fire, so will it be at the end of the age. ⁴¹ The Son of Man will send his angels, and they will collect out of his kingdom all causes of sin and all evildoers, ⁴² and they will throw them into the furnace of fire, where there will be weeping and gnashing of teeth. ⁴³ Then the righteous will shine like the sun in the kingdom of their Father. Let anyone with ears listen! ⁴⁴ "The kingdom of heaven is like treasure hidden in a field, which someone found and hid; then in his joy he goes and sells all that he has and buys that field. ⁴⁵ "Again, the kingdom of heaven is like a merchant in search of fine pearls; ⁴⁶ on finding one pearl of great value, he went and sold all that he had and bought it. ⁴⁷ "Again, the kingdom of heaven is like a net that was thrown into the sea and caught fish of every kind; ⁴⁸ when it was full, they drew it ashore, sat down, and put the good into baskets but threw out the bad. ⁴⁹ So it will be at the end of the age. The angels will come out and separate the evil from the righteous ⁵⁰ and throw them into the furnace of fire, where there will be weeping and gnashing of teeth. ⁵¹ "Have you understood all this?" They answered, "Yes." ⁵² And he said to them, "Therefore every scribe who has been trained for the kingdom of heaven is like the master of a household who brings out of his treasure what is new and what is old."

PETER WALKS ON WATER (14:28–31)

Greek

²⁸ ἀποκριθεὶς δὲ αὐτῷ ὁ Πέτρος εἶπεν, Κύριε, εἰ σὺ εἶ, κέλευσόν με ἐλθεῖν πρὸς σὲ ἐπὶ τὰ ὕδατα· ²⁹ ὁ δὲ εἶπεν, Ἐλθέ. καὶ καταβὰς ἀπὸ τοῦ πλοίου ὁ Πέτρος περιεπάτησεν ἐπὶ τὰ ὕδατα καὶ ἦλθεν πρὸς τὸν Ἰησοῦν. ³⁰ βλέπων δὲ τὸν ἄνεμον ἐφοβήθη, καὶ ἀρξάμενος καταποντίζεσθαι ἔκραξεν λέγων, Κύριε, σῶσόν με. ³¹ εὐθέως δὲ ὁ Ἰησοῦς ἐκτείνας τὴν χεῖρα ἐπελάβετο αὐτοῦ καὶ λέγει αὐτῷ, Ὀλιγόπιστε, εἰς τί ἐδίστασας;

English

²⁸ Peter answered him, "Lord, if it is you, command me to come to you on the water." ²⁹ He said, "Come." So Peter got out of the boat, started walking on the water, and came toward Jesus. ³⁰ But when he noticed the strong wind, he became frightened, and beginning to sink, he cried out, "Lord, save me!" ³¹ Jesus immediately reached out his hand and caught him, saying to him, "You of little faith, why did you doubt?"

JESUS BLESSES PETER (16:17–19)

Greek

¹⁷ ἀποκριθεὶς δὲ ὁ Ἰησοῦς εἶπεν αὐτῷ, Μακάριος εἶ, Σίμων Βαριωνᾶ, ὅτι σὰρξ καὶ αἷμα οὐκ ἀπεκάλυψέν σοι ἀλλ᾽ ὁ πατήρ μου ὁ ἐν τοῖς οὐρανοῖς. ¹⁸ κἀγὼ δέ σοι λέγω ὅτι σὺ εἶ Πέτρος, καὶ ἐπὶ ταύτῃ τῇ πέτρᾳ οἰκοδομήσω μου τὴν ἐκκλησίαν, καὶ πύλαι ᾅδου οὐ κατισχύσουσιν αὐτῆς. ¹⁹ δώσω σοι τὰς κλεῖδας τῆς βασιλείας τῶν οὐρανῶν, καὶ ὃ ἐὰν δήσῃς ἐπὶ τῆς γῆς ἔσται δεδεμένον ἐν τοῖς οὐρανοῖς, καὶ ὃ ἐὰν λύσῃς ἐπὶ τῆς γῆς ἔσται λελυμένον ἐν τοῖς οὐρανοῖς.

English

¹⁷ And Jesus answered him, "Blessed are you, Simon son of Jonah! For flesh and blood has not revealed this to you, but my Father in heaven. ¹⁸ And I tell you, you are Peter, and on this rock I will build my church, and the gates of Hades will not prevail against it. ¹⁹ I will give you the keys of the kingdom of heaven, and whatever you bind on earth will be bound in heaven, and whatever you loose on earth will be loosed in heaven."

JESUS AND TEMPLE TAX (17:24–27)

Greek

²⁴ Ἐλθόντων δὲ αὐτῶν εἰς Καφαρναοὺμ προσῆλθον οἱ τὰ δίδραχμα λαμβάνοντες τῷ Πέτρῳ καὶ εἶπαν, Ὁ διδάσκαλος ὑμῶν οὐ τελεῖ τὰ δίδραχμα; ²⁵ λέγει, Ναί. καὶ ἐλθόντα εἰς τὴν οἰκίαν προέφθασεν αὐτὸν ὁ Ἰησοῦς λέγων, Τί σοι δοκεῖ, Σίμων; οἱ βασιλεῖς τῆς γῆς ἀπὸ τίνων λαμβάνουσιν τέλη ἢ κῆνσον; ἀπὸ τῶν υἱῶν αὐτῶν ἢ ἀπὸ τῶν ἀλλοτρίων; ²⁶ εἰπόντος δέ, Ἀπὸ τῶν ἀλλοτρίων, ἔφη αὐτῷ ὁ Ἰησοῦς, Ἄρα γε ἐλεύθεροί εἰσιν οἱ υἱοί. ²⁷ ἵνα δὲ μὴ σκανδαλίσωμεν αὐτούς, πορευθεὶς εἰς θάλασσαν βάλε ἄγκιστρον καὶ τὸν ἀναβάντα πρῶτον ἰχθὺν ἆρον, καὶ ἀνοίξας τὸ στόμα αὐτοῦ εὑρήσεις στατῆρα· ἐκεῖνον λαβὼν δὸς αὐτοῖς ἀντὶ ἐμοῦ καὶ σοῦ.

English

²⁴ When they reached Capernaum, the collectors of the temple tax came to Peter and said, "Does your teacher not pay the temple tax?" ²⁵ He said, "Yes, he does." And when he came home, Jesus spoke of it first, asking, "What do you think, Simon? From whom do kings of the earth take toll or tribute? From their children or from others?" ²⁶ When Peter said, "From others," Jesus said to him, "Then the children are free. ²⁷ However, so that we do not give offense to them, go to the sea and cast a hook; take the first fish that comes up; and when you open its mouth, you will find a coin; take that and give it to them for you and me."

REPROVING ONE WHO SINS (18:15–20)

Greek

¹⁵ Ἐὰν δὲ ἁμαρτήσῃ [εἰς σὲ] ὁ ἀδελφός σου, ὕπαγε ἔλεγξον αὐτὸν μεταξὺ σοῦ καὶ αὐτοῦ μόνου. ἐάν σου ἀκούσῃ, ἐκέρδησας τὸν ἀδελφόν σου· ¹⁶ ἐὰν δὲ μὴ ἀκούσῃ, παράλαβε μετὰ σοῦ ἔτι ἕνα ἢ δύο, ἵνα ἐπὶ στόματος δύο μαρτύρων ἢ τριῶν σταθῇ πᾶν ῥῆμα· ¹⁷ ἐὰν δὲ παρακούσῃ αὐτῶν, εἰπὲ τῇ ἐκκλησίᾳ· ἐὰν δὲ καὶ τῆς ἐκκλησίας παρακούσῃ, ἔστω σοι ὥσπερ ὁ ἐθνικὸς καὶ ὁ τελώνης. ¹⁸ Ἀμὴν λέγω ὑμῖν, ὅσα ἐὰν δήσητε ἐπὶ τῆς γῆς ἔσται δεδεμένα ἐν οὐρανῷ καὶ ὅσα ἐὰν λύσητε ἐπὶ τῆς γῆς ἔσται λελυμένα ἐν οὐρανῷ. ¹⁹ Πάλιν λέγω ὑμῖν ὅτι ἐὰν δύο συμφωνήσωσιν ἐξ ὑμῶν ἐπὶ τῆς γῆς περὶ παντὸς πράγματος οὗ ἐὰν αἰτήσωνται, γενήσεται αὐτοῖς παρὰ τοῦ

πατρός μου τοῦ ἐν οὐρανοῖς. ²⁰ οὗ γάρ εἰσιν δύο ἢ τρεῖς συνηγμένοι εἰς τὸ ἐμὸν ὄνομα, ἐκεῖ εἰμι ἐν μέσῳ αὐτῶν.

English

¹⁵ "If another member of the church sins against you, go and point out the fault when the two of you are alone. If the member listens to you, you have regained that one. ¹⁶ But if you are not listened to, take one or two others along with you, so that every word may be confirmed by the evidence of two or three witnesses. ¹⁷ If the member refuses to listen to them, tell it to the church; and if the offender refuses to listen even to the church, let such a one be to you as a Gentile and a tax collector. ¹⁸ Truly I tell you, whatever you bind on earth will be bound in heaven, and whatever you loose on earth will be loosed in heaven. ¹⁹ Again, truly I tell you, if two of you agree on earth about anything you ask, it will be done for you by my Father in heaven. ²⁰ For where two or three are gathered in my name, I am there among them."

PETER'S QUESTION ABOUT FORGIVENESS (18:21-22)

Greek

²¹ Τότε προσελθὼν ὁ Πέτρος εἶπεν αὐτῷ, Κύριε, ποσάκις ἁμαρτήσει εἰς ἐμὲ ὁ ἀδελφός μου καὶ ἀφήσω αὐτῷ; ἕως ἑπτάκις; ²² λέγει αὐτῷ ὁ Ἰησοῦς, Οὐ λέγω σοι ἕως ἑπτάκις ἀλλὰ ἕως ἑβδομηκοντάκις ἑπτά.

English

²¹ Then Peter came and said to him, "Lord, if another member of the church sins against me, how often should I forgive? As many as seven times?" ²² Jesus said to him, "Not seven times, but, I tell you, seventy-seven times."

PARABLE OF UNFORGIVING SERVANT (18:23-35)

Greek

²³ Διὰ τοῦτο ὡμοιώθη ἡ βασιλεία τῶν οὐρανῶν ἀνθρώπῳ βασιλεῖ ὃς ἠθέλησεν συνᾶραι λόγον μετὰ τῶν δούλων αὐτοῦ. ²⁴ ἀρξαμένου δὲ αὐτοῦ συναίρειν προσηνέχθη αὐτῷ εἷς ὀφειλέτης μυρίων ταλάντων. ²⁵ μὴ ἔχοντος δὲ αὐτοῦ ἀποδοῦναι ἐκέλευσεν αὐτὸν ὁ κύριος πραθῆναι καὶ τὴν γυναῖκα

καὶ τὰ τέκνα καὶ πάντα ὅσα ἔχει, καὶ ἀποδοθῆναι. ²⁶ πεσὼν οὖν ὁ δοῦλος προσεκύνει αὐτῷ λέγων, Μακροθύμησον ἐπ' ἐμοί, καὶ πάντα ἀποδώσω σοι. ²⁷ σπλαγχνισθεὶς δὲ ὁ κύριος τοῦ δούλου ἐκείνου ἀπέλυσεν αὐτόν, καὶ τὸ δάνειον ἀφῆκεν αὐτῷ. ²⁸ ἐξελθὼν δὲ ὁ δοῦλος ἐκεῖνος εὗρεν ἕνα τῶν συνδούλων αὐτοῦ ὃς ὤφειλεν αὐτῷ ἑκατὸν δηνάρια, καὶ κρατήσας αὐτὸν ἔπνιγεν λέγων, Ἀπόδος εἴ τι ὀφείλεις. ²⁹ πεσὼν οὖν ὁ σύνδουλος αὐτοῦ παρεκάλει αὐτὸν λέγων, Μακροθύμησον ἐπ' ἐμοί, καὶ ἀποδώσω σοι. ³⁰ ὁ δὲ οὐκ ἤθελεν, ἀλλὰ ἀπελθὼν ἔβαλεν αὐτὸν εἰς φυλακὴν ἕως ἀποδῷ τὸ ὀφειλόμενον. ³¹ ἰδόντες οὖν οἱ σύνδουλοι αὐτοῦ τὰ γενόμενα ἐλυπήθησαν σφόδρα, καὶ ἐλθόντες διεσάφησαν τῷ κυρίῳ ἑαυτῶν πάντα τὰ γενόμενα. ³² τότε προσκαλεσάμενος αὐτὸν ὁ κύριος αὐτοῦ λέγει αὐτῷ, Δοῦλε πονηρέ, πᾶσαν τὴν ὀφειλὴν ἐκείνην ἀφῆκά σοι, ἐπεὶ παρεκάλεσάς με· ³³ οὐκ ἔδει καὶ σὲ ἐλεῆσαι τὸν σύνδουλόν σου, ὡς κἀγὼ σὲ ἠλέησα; ³⁴ καὶ ὀργισθεὶς ὁ κύριος αὐτοῦ παρέδωκεν αὐτὸν τοῖς βασανισταῖς ἕως οὗ ἀποδῷ πᾶν τὸ ὀφειλόμενον. ³⁵ Οὕτως καὶ ὁ πατήρ μου ὁ οὐράνιος ποιήσει ὑμῖν ἐὰν μὴ ἀφῆτε ἕκαστος τῷ ἀδελφῷ αὐτοῦ ἀπὸ τῶν καρδιῶν ὑμῶν.

English

²³ "For this reason the kingdom of heaven may be compared to a king who wished to settle accounts with his slaves. ²⁴ When he began the reckoning, one who owed him ten thousand talents was brought to him; ²⁵ and, as he could not pay, his lord ordered him to be sold, together with his wife and children and all his possessions, and payment to be made. ²⁶ So the slave fell on his knees before him, saying, 'Have patience with me, and I will pay you everything.' ²⁷ And out of pity for him, the lord of that slave released him and forgave him the debt. ²⁸ But that same slave, as he went out, came upon one of his fellow slaves who owed him a hundred denarii; and seizing him by the throat, he said, 'Pay what you owe.' ²⁹ Then his fellow slave fell down and pleaded with him, 'Have patience with me, and I will pay you.' ³⁰ But he refused; then he went and threw him into prison until he would pay the debt. ³¹ When his fellow slaves saw what had happened, they were greatly distressed, and they went and reported to their lord all that had taken place. ³² Then his lord summoned him and said to him, 'You wicked slave! I forgave you all that debt because you pleaded with me. ³³ Should you not have had mercy on your fellow slave, as I had mercy on you?' ³⁴ And in anger his lord handed him over to be tortured until he would pay his entire debt. ³⁵ So my heavenly Father will also do to every one of you, if you do not forgive your brother or sister from your heart."

PARABLE OF LABORERS IN THE VINEYARD (20:1–16)

Greek

¹ Ὁμοία γάρ ἐστιν ἡ βασιλεία τῶν οὐρανῶν ἀνθρώπῳ οἰκοδεσπότῃ ὅστις ἐξῆλθεν ἅμα πρωῒ μισθώσασθαι ἐργάτας εἰς τὸν ἀμπελῶνα αὐτοῦ· ² συμφωνήσας δὲ μετὰ τῶν ἐργατῶν ἐκ δηναρίου τὴν ἡμέραν ἀπέστειλεν αὐτοὺς εἰς τὸν ἀμπελῶνα αὐτοῦ. ³ καὶ ἐξελθὼν περὶ τρίτην ὥραν εἶδεν ἄλλους ἑστῶτας ἐν τῇ ἀγορᾷ ἀργούς· ⁴ καὶ ἐκείνοις εἶπεν, Ὑπάγετε καὶ ὑμεῖς εἰς τὸν ἀμπελῶνα, καὶ ὃ ἐὰν ᾖ δίκαιον δώσω ὑμῖν. ⁵ οἱ δὲ ἀπῆλθον. πάλιν [δὲ] ἐξελθὼν περὶ ἕκτην καὶ ἐνάτην ὥραν ἐποίησεν ὡσαύτως. ⁶ περὶ δὲ τὴν ἑνδεκάτην ἐξελθὼν εὗρεν ἄλλους ἑστῶτας, καὶ λέγει αὐτοῖς, Τί ὧδε ἑστήκατε ὅλην τὴν ἡμέραν ἀργοί; ⁷ λέγουσιν αὐτῷ, Ὅτι οὐδεὶς ἡμᾶς ἐμισθώσατο. λέγει αὐτοῖς, Ὑπάγετε καὶ ὑμεῖς εἰς τὸν ἀμπελῶνα. ⁸ ὀψίας δὲ γενομένης λέγει ὁ κύριος τοῦ ἀμπελῶνος τῷ ἐπιτρόπῳ αὐτοῦ, Κάλεσον τοὺς ἐργάτας καὶ ἀπόδος αὐτοῖς τὸν μισθὸν ἀρξάμενος ἀπὸ τῶν ἐσχάτων ἕως τῶν πρώτων. ⁹ καὶ ἐλθόντες οἱ περὶ τὴν ἑνδεκάτην ὥραν ἔλαβον ἀνὰ δηνάριον. ¹⁰ καὶ ἐλθόντες οἱ πρῶτοι ἐνόμισαν ὅτι πλεῖον λήμψονται· καὶ ἔλαβον [τὸ] ἀνὰ δηνάριον καὶ αὐτοί. ¹¹ λαβόντες δὲ ἐγόγγυζον κατὰ τοῦ οἰκοδεσπότου ¹² λέγοντες, Οὗτοι οἱ ἔσχατοι μίαν ὥραν ἐποίησαν, καὶ ἴσους ἡμῖν αὐτοὺς ἐποίησας τοῖς βαστάσασι τὸ βάρος τῆς ἡμέρας καὶ τὸν καύσωνα. ¹³ ὁ δὲ ἀποκριθεὶς ἑνὶ αὐτῶν εἶπεν, Ἑταῖρε, οὐκ ἀδικῶ σε· οὐχὶ δηναρίου συνεφώνησάς μοι; ¹⁴ ἆρον τὸ σὸν καὶ ὕπαγε· θέλω δὲ τούτῳ τῷ ἐσχάτῳ δοῦναι ὡς καὶ σοί. ¹⁵ [ἢ] οὐκ ἔξεστίν μοι ὃ θέλω ποιῆσαι ἐν τοῖς ἐμοῖς; ἢ ὁ ὀφθαλμός σου πονηρός ἐστιν ὅτι ἐγὼ ἀγαθός εἰμι; ¹⁶ Οὕτως ἔσονται οἱ ἔσχατοι πρῶτοι καὶ οἱ πρῶτοι ἔσχατοι.

English

¹ "For the kingdom of heaven is like a landowner who went out early in the morning to hire laborers for his vineyard. ² After agreeing with the laborers for the usual daily wage, he sent them into his vineyard. ³ When he went out about nine o'clock, he saw others standing idle in the marketplace; ⁴ and he said to them, 'You also go into the vineyard, and I will pay you whatever is right.' So they went. ⁵ When he went out again about noon and about three o'clock, he did the same. ⁶ And about five o'clock he went out and found others standing around; and he said to them, 'Why are you standing here idle all day?' ⁷ They said to him, 'Because no one has hired us.' He said to them, 'You also go into the vineyard.'

⁸ When evening came, the owner of the vineyard said to his manager, 'Call the laborers and give them their pay, beginning with the last and then going to the first.' ⁹ When those hired about five o'clock came, each of them received the usual daily wage. ¹⁰ Now when the first came, they thought they would receive more; but each of them also received the usual daily wage. ¹¹ And when they received it, they grumbled against the landowner, ¹² saying, 'These last worked only one hour, and you have made them equal to us who have borne the burden of the day and the scorching heat.' ¹³ But he replied to one of them, 'Friend, I am doing you no wrong; did you not agree with me for the usual daily wage? ¹⁴ Take what belongs to you and go; I choose to give to this last the same as I give to you. ¹⁵ Am I not allowed to do what I choose with what belongs to me? Or are you envious because I am generous?' ¹⁶ So the last will be first, and the first will be last."

PARABLE OF TWO SONS (21:28–32)

Greek

²⁸ Τί δὲ ὑμῖν δοκεῖ; ἄνθρωπος εἶχεν τέκνα δύο. καὶ προσελθὼν τῷ πρώτῳ εἶπεν, Τέκνον, ὕπαγε σήμερον ἐργάζου ἐν τῷ ἀμπελῶνι. ²⁹ ὁ δὲ ἀποκριθεὶς εἶπεν, Οὐ θέλω, ὕστερον δὲ μεταμεληθεὶς ἀπῆλθεν. ³⁰ προσελθὼν δὲ τῷ ἑτέρῳ εἶπεν ὡσαύτως. ὁ δὲ ἀποκριθεὶς εἶπεν, Ἐγώ, κύριε· καὶ οὐκ ἀπῆλθεν. ³¹ τίς ἐκ τῶν δύο ἐποίησεν τὸ θέλημα τοῦ πατρός; λέγουσιν, Ὁ πρῶτος. λέγει αὐτοῖς ὁ Ἰησοῦς, Ἀμὴν λέγω ὑμῖν ὅτι οἱ τελῶναι καὶ αἱ πόρναι προάγουσιν ὑμᾶς εἰς τὴν βασιλείαν τοῦ θεοῦ. ³² ἦλθεν γὰρ Ἰωάννης πρὸς ὑμᾶς ἐν ὁδῷ δικαιοσύνης, καὶ οὐκ ἐπιστεύσατε αὐτῷ· οἱ δὲ τελῶναι καὶ αἱ πόρναι ἐπίστευσαν αὐτῷ· ὑμεῖς δὲ ἰδόντες οὐδὲ μετεμελήθητε ὕστερον τοῦ πιστεῦσαι αὐτῷ.

English

²⁸ "What do you think? A man had two sons; he went to the first and said, 'Son, go and work in the vineyard today.' ²⁹ He answered, 'I will not'; but later he changed his mind and went. ³⁰ The father went to the second and said the same; and he answered, 'I go, sir'; but he did not go. ³¹ Which of the two did the will of his father?" They said, "The first." Jesus said to them, "Truly I tell you, the tax collectors and the prostitutes are going into the kingdom of God ahead of you. ³² For John came to you in the

way of righteousness and you did not believe him, but the tax collectors and the prostitutes believed him; and even after you saw it, you did not change your minds and believe him."

PROHIBITION OF TITLES (23:2–5, 7–12)

Greek

² Ἐπὶ τῆς Μωϋσέως καθέδρας ἐκάθισαν οἱ γραμματεῖς καὶ οἱ Φαρισαῖοι. ³ πάντα οὖν ὅσα ἐὰν εἴπωσιν ὑμῖν ποιήσατε καὶ τηρεῖτε, κατὰ δὲ τὰ ἔργα αὐτῶν μὴ ποιεῖτε· λέγουσιν γὰρ καὶ οὐ ποιοῦσιν. ⁴ δεσμεύουσιν δὲ φορτία βαρέα καὶ ἐπιτιθέασιν ἐπὶ τοὺς ὤμους τῶν ἀνθρώπων, αὐτοὶ δὲ τῷ δακτύλῳ αὐτῶν οὐ θέλουσιν κινῆσαι αὐτά. ⁵ πάντα δὲ τὰ ἔργα αὐτῶν ποιοῦσιν πρὸς τὸ θεαθῆναι τοῖς ἀνθρώποις· πλατύνουσιν γὰρ τὰ φυλακτήρια αὐτῶν καὶ μεγαλύνουσιν τὰ κράσπεδα.

⁷ καὶ τοὺς ἀσπασμοὺς ἐν ταῖς ἀγοραῖς καὶ καλεῖσθαι ὑπὸ τῶν ἀνθρώπων, Ῥαββί. ⁸ ὑμεῖς δὲ μὴ κληθῆτε, Ῥαββί, εἷς γάρ ἐστιν ὑμῶν ὁ διδάσκαλος, πάντες δὲ ὑμεῖς ἀδελφοί ἐστε. ⁹ καὶ πατέρα μὴ καλέσητε ὑμῖν ἐπὶ τῆς γῆς, εἷς γάρ ἐστιν ὑμῶν ὁ πατὴρ ὁ οὐράνιος. ¹⁰ μηδὲ κληθῆτε καθηγηταί, ὅτι καθηγητὴς ὑμῶν ἐστιν εἷς ὁ Χριστός. ¹¹ ὁ δὲ μείζων ὑμῶν ἔσται ὑμῶν διάκονος. ¹² ὅστις δὲ ὑψώσει ἑαυτὸν ταπεινωθήσεται, καὶ ὅστις ταπεινώσει ἑαυτὸν ὑψωθήσεται.

English

² "The scribes and the Pharisees sit on Moses' seat; ³ therefore, do whatever they teach you and follow it; but do not do as they do, for they do not practice what they teach. ⁴ They tie up heavy burdens, hard to bear, and lay them on the shoulders of others; but they themselves are unwilling to lift a finger to move them. ⁵ They do all their deeds to be seen by others; for they make their phylacteries broad and their fringes long."
⁷ ". . . and to be greeted with respect in the marketplaces, and to have people call them rabbi. ⁸ But you are not to be called rabbi, for you have one teacher, and you are all students. ⁹ And call no one your father on earth, for you have one Father—the one in heaven. ¹⁰ Nor are you to be called instructors, for you have one instructor, the Messiah. ¹¹ The greatest among you will be your servant. ¹² All who exalt themselves will be humbled, and all who humble themselves will be exalted."

JESUS DENOUNCES THE SCRIBES AND PHARISEES
(23:15–22)

Greek

¹⁵ Οὐαὶ ὑμῖν, γραμματεῖς καὶ Φαρισαῖοι ὑποκριταί, ὅτι περιάγετε τὴν θάλασσαν καὶ τὴν ξηρὰν ποιῆσαι ἕνα προσήλυτον, καὶ ὅταν γένηται ποιεῖτε αὐτὸν υἱὸν γεέννης διπλότερον ὑμῶν. ¹⁶ Οὐαὶ ὑμῖν, ὁδηγοὶ τυφλοὶ οἱ λέγοντες, Ὃς ἂν ὀμόσῃ ἐν τῷ ναῷ, οὐδέν ἐστιν· ὃς δ᾽ ἂν ὀμόσῃ ἐν τῷ χρυσῷ τοῦ ναοῦ ὀφείλει. ¹⁷ μωροὶ καὶ τυφλοί, τίς γὰρ μείζων ἐστίν, ὁ χρυσὸς ἢ ὁ ναὸς ὁ ἁγιάσας τὸν χρυσόν; ¹⁸ καί, Ὃς ἂν ὀμόσῃ ἐν τῷ θυσιαστηρίῳ, οὐδέν ἐστιν· ὃς δ᾽ ἂν ὀμόσῃ ἐν τῷ δώρῳ τῷ ἐπάνω αὐτοῦ ὀφείλει. ¹⁹ τυφλοί, τί γὰρ μεῖζον, τὸ δῶρον ἢ τὸ θυσιαστήριον τὸ ἁγιάζον τὸ δῶρον; ²⁰ ὁ οὖν ὀμόσας ἐν τῷ θυσιαστηρίῳ ὀμνύει ἐν αὐτῷ καὶ ἐν πᾶσι τοῖς ἐπάνω αὐτοῦ· ²¹ καὶ ὁ ὀμόσας ἐν τῷ ναῷ ὀμνύει ἐν αὐτῷ καὶ ἐν τῷ κατοικοῦντι αὐτόν· ²² καὶ ὁ ὀμόσας ἐν τῷ οὐρανῷ ὀμνύει ἐν τῷ θρόνῳ τοῦ θεοῦ καὶ ἐν τῷ καθημένῳ ἐπάνω αὐτοῦ.

English

¹⁵ Woe to you, scribes and Pharisees, hypocrites! For you cross sea and land to make a single convert, and you make the new convert twice as much a child of hell as yourselves. ¹⁶ "Woe to you, blind guides, who say, 'Whoever swears by the sanctuary is bound by nothing, but whoever swears by the gold of the sanctuary is bound by the oath.' ¹⁷ You blind fools! For which is greater, the gold or the sanctuary that has made the gold sacred? ¹⁸ And you say, 'Whoever swears by the altar is bound by nothing, but whoever swears by the gift that is on the altar is bound by the oath.' ¹⁹ How blind you are! For which is greater, the gift or the altar that makes the gift sacred? ²⁰ So whoever swears by the altar, swears by it and by everything on it; ²¹ and whoever swears by the sanctuary, swears by it and by the one who dwells in it; ²² and whoever swears by heaven, swears by the throne of God and by the one who is seated upon it."

PARABLE OF THE TEN BRIDESMAIDS (25:1–13)

Greek

¹ Τότε ὁμοιωθήσεται ἡ βασιλεία τῶν οὐρανῶν δέκα παρθένοις, αἵτινες λαβοῦσαι τὰς λαμπάδας ἑαυτῶν ἐξῆλθον εἰς ὑπάντησιν τοῦ νυμφίου. ² πέντε δὲ ἐξ αὐτῶν ἦσαν μωραὶ καὶ πέντε φρόνιμοι. ³ αἱ γὰρ μωραὶ λαβοῦσαι τὰς λαμπάδας αὐτῶν οὐκ ἔλαβον μεθ᾽ ἑαυτῶν ἔλαιον· ⁴ αἱ δὲ φρόνιμοι ἔλαβον ἔλαιον ἐν τοῖς ἀγγείοις μετὰ τῶν λαμπάδων ἑαυτῶν. ⁵ χρονίζοντος δὲ τοῦ νυμφίου ἐνύσταξαν πᾶσαι καὶ ἐκάθευδον. ⁶ μέσης δὲ νυκτὸς κραυγὴ γέγονεν, Ἰδοὺ ὁ νυμφίος, ἐξέρχεσθε εἰς ἀπάντησιν αὐτοῦ. ⁷ τότε ἠγέρθησαν πᾶσαι αἱ παρθένοι ἐκεῖναι καὶ ἐκόσμησαν τὰς λαμπάδας ἑαυτῶν. ⁸ αἱ δὲ μωραὶ ταῖς φρονίμοις εἶπαν, Δότε ἡμῖν ἐκ τοῦ ἐλαίου ὑμῶν, ὅτι αἱ λαμπάδες ἡμῶν σβέννυνται. ⁹ ἀπεκρίθησαν δὲ αἱ φρόνιμοι λέγουσαι, Μήποτε οὐκ ἀρκέσῃ ἡμῖν καὶ ὑμῖν· πορεύεσθε μᾶλλον πρὸς τοὺς πωλοῦντας καὶ ἀγοράσατε ἑαυταῖς. ¹⁰ ἀπερχομένων δὲ αὐτῶν ἀγοράσαι ἦλθεν ὁ νυμφίος, καὶ αἱ ἕτοιμοι εἰσῆλθον μετ᾽ αὐτοῦ εἰς τοὺς γάμους, καὶ ἐκλείσθη ἡ θύρα. ¹¹ ὕστερον δὲ ἔρχονται καὶ αἱ λοιπαὶ παρθένοι λέγουσαι, Κύριε κύριε, ἄνοιξον ἡμῖν. ¹² ὁ δὲ ἀποκριθεὶς εἶπεν, Ἀμὴν λέγω ὑμῖν, οὐκ οἶδα ὑμᾶς. ¹³ Γρηγορεῖτε οὖν, ὅτι οὐκ οἴδατε τὴν ἡμέραν οὐδὲ τὴν ὥραν.

English

¹ "Then the kingdom of heaven will be like this. Ten bridesmaids took their lamps and went to meet the bridegroom. ² Five of them were foolish, and five were wise. ³ When the foolish took their lamps, they took no oil with them; ⁴ but the wise took flasks of oil with their lamps. ⁵ As the bridegroom was delayed, all of them became drowsy and slept. ⁶ But at midnight there was a shout, 'Look! Here is the bridegroom! Come out to meet him.' ⁷ Then all those bridesmaids got up and trimmed their lamps. ⁸ The foolish said to the wise, 'Give us some of your oil, for our lamps are going out.' ⁹ But the wise replied, 'No! there will not be enough for you and for us; you had better go to the dealers and buy some for yourselves.' ¹⁰ And while they went to buy it, the bridegroom came, and those who were ready went with him into the wedding banquet; and the door was shut. ¹¹ Later the other bridesmaids came also, saying, 'Lord, lord, open to us.' ¹² But he replied, 'Truly I tell you, I do not know you.' ¹³ Keep awake therefore, for you know neither the day nor the hour."

SHEEP AND GOATS (25:31–46)

Greek

³¹ "Ὅταν δὲ ἔλθῃ ὁ υἱὸς τοῦ ἀνθρώπου ἐν τῇ δόξῃ αὐτοῦ καὶ πάντες οἱ ἄγγελοι μετ' αὐτοῦ, τότε καθίσει ἐπὶ θρόνου δόξης αὐτοῦ· ³² καὶ συναχθήσονται ἔμπροσθεν αὐτοῦ πάντα τὰ ἔθνη, καὶ ἀφορίσει αὐτοὺς ἀπ' ἀλλήλων, ὥσπερ ὁ ποιμὴν ἀφορίζει τὰ πρόβατα ἀπὸ τῶν ἐρίφων, ³³ καὶ στήσει τὰ μὲν πρόβατα ἐκ δεξιῶν αὐτοῦ τὰ δὲ ἐρίφια ἐξ εὐωνύμων. ³⁴ τότε ἐρεῖ ὁ βασιλεὺς τοῖς ἐκ δεξιῶν αὐτοῦ, Δεῦτε, οἱ εὐλογημένοι τοῦ πατρός μου, κληρονομήσατε τὴν ἡτοιμασμένην ὑμῖν βασιλείαν ἀπὸ καταβολῆς κόσμου· ³⁵ ἐπείνασα γὰρ καὶ ἐδώκατέ μοι φαγεῖν, ἐδίψησα καὶ ἐποτίσατέ με, ξένος ἤμην καὶ συνηγάγετέ με, ³⁶ γυμνὸς καὶ περιεβάλετέ με, ἠσθένησα καὶ ἐπεσκέψασθέ με, ἐν φυλακῇ ἤμην καὶ ἤλθατε πρός με. ³⁷ τότε ἀποκριθήσονται αὐτῷ οἱ δίκαιοι λέγοντες, Κύριε, πότε σε εἴδομεν πεινῶντα καὶ ἐθρέψαμεν, ἢ διψῶντα καὶ ἐποτίσαμεν; ³⁸ πότε δέ σε εἴδομεν ξένον καὶ συνηγάγομεν, ἢ γυμνὸν καὶ περιεβάλομεν; ³⁹ πότε δέ σε εἴδομεν ἀσθενοῦντα ἢ ἐν φυλακῇ καὶ ἤλθομεν πρός σε; ⁴⁰ καὶ ἀποκριθεὶς ὁ βασιλεὺς ἐρεῖ αὐτοῖς, Ἀμὴν λέγω ὑμῖν, ἐφ' ὅσον ἐποιήσατε ἑνὶ τούτων τῶν ἀδελφῶν μου τῶν ἐλαχίστων, ἐμοὶ ἐποιήσατε. ⁴¹ Τότε ἐρεῖ καὶ τοῖς ἐξ εὐωνύμων, Πορεύεσθε ἀπ' ἐμοῦ [οἱ] κατηραμένοι εἰς τὸ πῦρ τὸ αἰώνιον τὸ ἡτοιμασμένον τῷ διαβόλῳ καὶ τοῖς ἀγγέλοις αὐτοῦ· ⁴² ἐπείνασα γὰρ καὶ οὐκ ἐδώκατέ μοι φαγεῖν, ἐδίψησα καὶ οὐκ ἐποτίσατέ με, ⁴³ ξένος ἤμην καὶ οὐ συνηγάγετέ με, γυμνὸς καὶ οὐ περιεβάλετέ με, ἀσθενὴς καὶ ἐν φυλακῇ καὶ οὐκ ἐπεσκέψασθέ με. ⁴⁴ τότε ἀποκριθήσονται καὶ αὐτοὶ λέγοντες, Κύριε, πότε σε εἴδομεν πεινῶντα ἢ διψῶντα ἢ ξένον ἢ γυμνὸν ἢ ἀσθενῆ ἢ ἐν φυλακῇ καὶ οὐ διηκονήσαμέν σοι; ⁴⁵ τότε ἀποκριθήσεται αὐτοῖς λέγων, Ἀμὴν λέγω ὑμῖν, ἐφ' ὅσον οὐκ ἐποιήσατε ἑνὶ τούτων τῶν ἐλαχίστων, οὐδὲ ἐμοὶ ἐποιήσατε. ⁴⁶ καὶ ἀπελεύσονται οὗτοι εἰς κόλασιν αἰώνιον, οἱ δὲ δίκαιοι εἰς ζωὴν αἰώνιον.

English

³¹ "When the Son of Man comes in his glory, and all the angels with him, then he will sit on the throne of his glory. ³² All the nations will be gathered before him, and he will separate people one from another as a shepherd separates the sheep from the goats, ³³ and he will put the sheep at his right hand and the goats at the left. ³⁴ Then the king will say to those at his right hand, 'Come, you that are blessed by my Father, inherit the kingdom prepared for you from the foundation of the world;

³⁵ for I was hungry and you gave me food, I was thirsty and you gave me something to drink, I was a stranger and you welcomed me, ³⁶ I was naked and you gave me clothing, I was sick and you took care of me, I was in prison and you visited me.' ³⁷ Then the righteous will answer him, 'Lord, when was it that we saw you hungry and gave you food, or thirsty and gave you something to drink? ³⁸ And when was it that we saw you a stranger and welcomed you, or naked and gave you clothing? ³⁹ And when was it that we saw you sick or in prison and visited you?' ⁴⁰ And the king will answer them, 'Truly I tell you, just as you did it to one of the least of these who are members of my family, you did it to me.' ⁴¹ Then he will say to those at his left hand, 'You that are accursed, depart from me into the eternal fire prepared for the devil and his angels; ⁴² for I was hungry and you gave me no food, I was thirsty and you gave me nothing to drink, ⁴³ I was a stranger and you did not welcome me, naked and you did not give me clothing, sick and in prison and you did not visit me.' ⁴⁴ Then they also will answer, 'Lord, when was it that we saw you hungry or thirsty or a stranger or naked or sick or in prison, and did not take care of you?' ⁴⁵ Then he will answer them, 'Truly I tell you, just as you did not do it to one of the least of these, you did not do it to me.' ⁴⁶ And these will go away into eternal punishment, but the righteous into eternal life."

DEATH OF JUDAS (27:3-10)

Greek

³ Τότε ἰδὼν Ἰούδας ὁ παραδιδοὺς αὐτὸν ὅτι κατεκρίθη μεταμεληθεὶς ἔστρεψεν τὰ τριάκοντα ἀργύρια τοῖς ἀρχιερεῦσιν καὶ πρεσβυτέροις ⁴ λέγων, Ἥμαρτον παραδοὺς αἷμα ἀθῷον. οἱ δὲ εἶπαν, Τί πρὸς ἡμᾶς; σὺ ὄψῃ. ⁵ καὶ ῥίψας τὰ ἀργύρια εἰς τὸν ναὸν ἀνεχώρησεν, καὶ ἀπελθὼν ἀπήγξατο. ⁶ οἱ δὲ ἀρχιερεῖς λαβόντες τὰ ἀργύρια εἶπαν, Οὐκ ἔξεστιν βαλεῖν αὐτὰ εἰς τὸν κορβανᾶν, ἐπεὶ τιμὴ αἵματός ἐστιν. ⁷ συμβούλιον δὲ λαβόντες ἠγόρασαν ἐξ αὐτῶν τὸν Ἀγρὸν τοῦ Κεραμέως εἰς ταφὴν τοῖς ξένοις. ⁸ διὸ ἐκλήθη ὁ ἀγρὸς ἐκεῖνος Ἀγρὸς Αἵματος ἕως τῆς σήμερον. ⁹ τότε ἐπληρώθη τὸ ῥηθὲν διὰ Ἰερεμίου τοῦ προφήτου λέγοντος, Καὶ ἔλαβον τὰ τριάκοντα ἀργύρια, τὴν τιμὴν τοῦ τετιμημένου ὃν ἐτιμήσαντο ἀπὸ υἱῶν Ἰσραήλ, ¹⁰ καὶ ἔδωκαν αὐτὰ εἰς τὸν ἀγρὸν τοῦ κεραμέως, καθὰ συνέταξέν μοι κύριος.

English

³ When Judas, his betrayer, saw that Jesus was condemned, he repented and brought back the thirty pieces of silver to the chief priests and the elders. ⁴ He said, "I have sinned by betraying innocent blood." But they said, "What is that to us? See to it yourself." ⁵ Throwing down the pieces of silver in the temple, he departed; and he went and hanged himself. ⁶ But the chief priests, taking the pieces of silver, said, "It is not lawful to put them into the treasury, since they are blood money." ⁷ After conferring together, they used them to buy the potter's field as a place to bury foreigners. ⁸ For this reason that field has been called the Field of Blood to this day. ⁹ Then was fulfilled what had been spoken through the prophet Jeremiah, "And they took the thirty pieces of silver, the price of the one on whom a price had been set, on whom some of the people of Israel had set a price, ¹⁰ and they gave them for the potter's field, as the Lord commanded me."

PILATE WASHES HIS HANDS (27:24–25)

Greek

²⁴ ἰδὼν δὲ ὁ Πιλᾶτος ὅτι οὐδὲν ὠφελεῖ ἀλλὰ μᾶλλον θόρυβος γίνεται, λαβὼν ὕδωρ ἀπενίψατο τὰς χεῖρας ἀπέναντι τοῦ ὄχλου, λέγων, Ἀθῷός εἰμι ἀπὸ τοῦ αἵματος τούτου· ὑμεῖς ὄψεσθε. ²⁵ καὶ ἀποκριθεὶς πᾶς ὁ λαὸς εἶπεν, Τὸ αἷμα αὐτοῦ ἐφ' ἡμᾶς καὶ ἐπὶ τὰ τέκνα ἡμῶν.

English

²⁴ So when Pilate saw that he could do nothing, but rather that a riot was beginning, he took some water and washed his hands before the crowd, saying, "I am innocent of this man's blood; see to it yourselves." ²⁵ Then the people as a whole answered, "His blood be on us and on our children!"

RESURRECTION OF SAINTS (27:52–53)

Greek

⁵² καὶ τὰ μνημεῖα ἀνεῴχθησαν καὶ πολλὰ σώματα τῶν κεκοιμημένων ἁγίων ἠγέρθησαν, ⁵³ καὶ ἐξελθόντες ἐκ τῶν μνημείων μετὰ τὴν ἔγερσιν αὐτοῦ εἰσῆλθον εἰς τὴν ἁγίαν πόλιν καὶ ἐνεφανίσθησαν πολλοῖς.

English

⁵² The tombs also were opened, and many bodies of the saints who had fallen asleep were raised. ⁵³ After his resurrection they came out of the tombs and entered the holy city and appeared to many.

GUARD AT THE TOMB (27:62–66)

Greek

⁶² Τῇ δὲ ἐπαύριον, ἥτις ἐστὶν μετὰ τὴν παρασκευήν, συνήχθησαν οἱ ἀρχιερεῖς καὶ οἱ Φαρισαῖοι πρὸς Πιλᾶτον ⁶³ λέγοντες, Κύριε, ἐμνήσθημεν ὅτι ἐκεῖνος ὁ πλάνος εἶπεν ἔτι ζῶν, Μετὰ τρεῖς ἡμέρας ἐγείρομαι. ⁶⁴ κέλευσον οὖν ἀσφαλισθῆναι τὸν τάφον ἕως τῆς τρίτης ἡμέρας, μήποτε ἐλθόντες οἱ μαθηταὶ αὐτοῦ κλέψωσιν αὐτὸν καὶ εἴπωσιν τῷ λαῷ, Ἠγέρθη ἀπὸ τῶν νεκρῶν, καὶ ἔσται ἡ ἐσχάτη πλάνη χείρων τῆς πρώτης. ⁶⁵ ἔφη αὐτοῖς ὁ Πιλᾶτος, Ἔχετε κουστωδίαν· ὑπάγετε ἀσφαλίσασθε ὡς οἴδατε. ⁶⁶ οἱ δὲ πορευθέντες ἠσφαλίσαντο τὸν τάφον σφραγίσαντες τὸν λίθον μετὰ τῆς κουστωδίας.

English

⁶² The next day, that is, after the day of Preparation, the chief priests and the Pharisees gathered before Pilate ⁶³ and said, "Sir, we remember what that impostor said while he was still alive, 'After three days I will rise again.' ⁶⁴ Therefore command the tomb to be made secure until the third day; otherwise his disciples may go and steal him away, and tell the people, 'He has been raised from the dead,' and the last deception would be worse than the first." ⁶⁵ Pilate said to them, "You have a guard of soldiers; go, make it as secure as you can." ⁶⁶ So they went with the guard and made the tomb secure by sealing the stone.

REPORT OF THE GUARD (28:11–15)

Greek

¹¹ Πορευομένων δὲ αὐτῶν ἰδού τινες τῆς κουστωδίας ἐλθόντες εἰς τὴν πόλιν ἀπήγγειλαν τοῖς ἀρχιερεῦσιν ἅπαντα τὰ γενόμενα. ¹² καὶ συναχθέντες μετὰ τῶν πρεσβυτέρων συμβούλιόν τε λαβόντες ἀργύρια ἱκανὰ ἔδωκαν τοῖς στρατιώταις ¹³ λέγοντες, Εἴπατε ὅτι Οἱ μαθηταὶ αὐτοῦ νυκτὸς ἐλθόντες ἔκλεψαν αὐτὸν ἡμῶν κοιμωμένων. ¹⁴ καὶ ἐὰν ἀκουσθῇ τοῦτο ἐπὶ τοῦ ἡγεμόνος, ἡμεῖς πείσομεν αὐτὸν καὶ ὑμᾶς ἀμερίμνους ποιήσομεν. ¹⁵ οἱ δὲ λαβόντες τὰ ἀργύρια ἐποίησαν ὡς ἐδιδάχθησαν. Καὶ διεφημίσθη ὁ λόγος οὗτος παρὰ Ἰουδαίοις μέχρι τῆς σήμερον [ἡμέρας].

English

¹¹ While they were going, some of the guard went into the city and told the chief priests everything that had happened. ¹² After the priests had assembled with the elders, they devised a plan to give a large sum of money to the soldiers, ¹³ telling them, "You must say, 'His disciples came by night and stole him away while we were asleep.' ¹⁴ If this comes to the governor's ears, we will satisfy him and keep you out of trouble." ¹⁵ So they took the money and did as they were directed. And this story is still told among the Jews to this day.

GREAT COMMISSION (28:16–20)

Greek

¹⁶ Οἱ δὲ ἕνδεκα μαθηταὶ ἐπορεύθησαν εἰς τὴν Γαλιλαίαν εἰς τὸ ὄρος οὗ ἐτάξατο αὐτοῖς ὁ Ἰησοῦς, ¹⁷ καὶ ἰδόντες αὐτὸν προσεκύνησαν, οἱ δὲ ἐδίστασαν. ¹⁸ καὶ προσελθὼν ὁ Ἰησοῦς ἐλάλησεν αὐτοῖς λέγων, Ἐδόθη μοι πᾶσα ἐξουσία ἐν οὐρανῷ καὶ ἐπὶ γῆς. ¹⁹ πορευθέντες οὖν μαθητεύσατε πάντα τὰ ἔθνη, βαπτίζοντες αὐτοὺς εἰς τὸ ὄνομα τοῦ πατρὸς καὶ τοῦ υἱοῦ καὶ τοῦ ἁγίου πνεύματος, ²⁰ διδάσκοντες αὐτοὺς τηρεῖν πάντα ὅσα ἐνετειλάμην ὑμῖν· καὶ ἰδοὺ ἐγὼ μεθ' ὑμῶν εἰμι πάσας τὰς ἡμέρας ἕως τῆς συντελείας τοῦ αἰῶνος.

English

[16] Now the eleven disciples went to Galilee, to the mountain to which Jesus had directed them. [17] When they saw him, they worshiped him; but some doubted. [18] And Jesus came and said to them, "All authority in heaven and on earth has been given to me. [19] Go therefore and make disciples of all nations, baptizing them in the name of the Father and of the Son and of the Holy Spirit, [20] and teaching them to obey everything that I have commanded you. And remember, I am with you always, to the end of the age."

3

Greek–English Texts of Luke's Unique Material

PROLOGUE (1:1-4)

Greek

¹ Ἐπειδήπερ πολλοὶ ἐπεχείρησαν ἀνατάξασθαι διήγησιν περὶ τῶν πεπληροφορημένων ἐν ἡμῖν πραγμάτων, ² καθὼς παρέδοσαν ἡμῖν οἱ ἀπ' ἀρχῆς αὐτόπται καὶ ὑπηρέται γενόμενοι τοῦ λόγου, ³ ἔδοξε κἀμοὶ παρηκολουθηκότι ἄνωθεν πᾶσιν ἀκριβῶς καθεξῆς σοι γράψαι, κράτιστε Θεόφιλε, ⁴ ἵνα ἐπιγνῷς περὶ ὧν κατηχήθης λόγων τὴν ἀσφάλειαν.

English

¹ Since many have undertaken to set down an orderly account of the events that have been fulfilled among us, ² just as they were handed on to us by those who from the beginning were eyewitnesses and servants of the word, ³ I too decided, after investigating everything carefully from the very first, to write an orderly account for you, most excellent Theophilus, ⁴ so that you may know the truth concerning the things about which you have been instructed.

BIRTH OF JOHN FORETOLD (1:5-25)

Greek

⁵ Ἐγένετο ἐν ταῖς ἡμέραις Ἡρῴδου βασιλέως τῆς Ἰουδαίας ἱερεύς τις ὀνόματι Ζαχαρίας ἐξ ἐφημερίας Ἀβιά, καὶ γυνὴ αὐτῷ ἐκ τῶν θυγατέρων Ἀαρών, καὶ τὸ ὄνομα αὐτῆς Ἐλισάβετ. ⁶ ἦσαν δὲ δίκαιοι ἀμφότεροι ἐναντίον τοῦ θεοῦ,

πορευόμενοι ἐν πάσαις ταῖς ἐντολαῖς καὶ δικαιώμασιν τοῦ κυρίου ἄμεμπτοι. ⁷ καὶ οὐκ ἦν αὐτοῖς τέκνον, καθότι ἦν ἡ Ἐλισάβετ στεῖρα, καὶ ἀμφότεροι προβεβηκότες ἐν ταῖς ἡμέραις αὐτῶν ἦσαν. ⁸ Ἐγένετο δὲ ἐν τῷ ἱερατεύειν αὐτὸν ἐν τῇ τάξει τῆς ἐφημερίας αὐτοῦ ἔναντι τοῦ θεοῦ, ⁹ κατὰ τὸ ἔθος τῆς ἱερατείας ἔλαχε τοῦ θυμιᾶσαι εἰσελθὼν εἰς τὸν ναὸν τοῦ κυρίου, ¹⁰ καὶ πᾶν τὸ πλῆθος ἦν τοῦ λαοῦ προσευχόμενον ἔξω τῇ ὥρᾳ τοῦ θυμιάματος· ¹¹ ὤφθη δὲ αὐτῷ ἄγγελος κυρίου ἑστὼς ἐκ δεξιῶν τοῦ θυσιαστηρίου τοῦ θυμιάματος. ¹² καὶ ἐταράχθη Ζαχαρίας ἰδών, καὶ φόβος ἐπέπεσεν ἐπ' αὐτόν. ¹³ εἶπεν δὲ πρὸς αὐτὸν ὁ ἄγγελος, Μὴ φοβοῦ, Ζαχαρία, διότι εἰσηκούσθη ἡ δέησίς σου, καὶ ἡ γυνή σου Ἐλισάβετ γεννήσει υἱόν σοι, καὶ καλέσεις τὸ ὄνομα αὐτοῦ Ἰωάννην. ¹⁴ καὶ ἔσται χαρά σοι καὶ ἀγαλλίασις, καὶ πολλοὶ ἐπὶ τῇ γενέσει αὐτοῦ χαρήσονται· ¹⁵ ἔσται γὰρ μέγας ἐνώπιον [τοῦ] κυρίου, καὶ οἶνον καὶ σίκερα οὐ μὴ πίῃ, καὶ πνεύματος ἁγίου πλησθήσεται ἔτι ἐκ κοιλίας μητρὸς αὐτοῦ, ¹⁶ καὶ πολλοὺς τῶν υἱῶν Ἰσραὴλ ἐπιστρέψει ἐπὶ κύριον τὸν θεὸν αὐτῶν. ¹⁷ καὶ αὐτὸς προελεύσεται ἐνώπιον αὐτοῦ ἐν πνεύματι καὶ δυνάμει Ἠλίου, ἐπιστρέψαι καρδίας πατέρων ἐπὶ τέκνα καὶ ἀπειθεῖς ἐν φρονήσει δικαίων, ἑτοιμάσαι κυρίῳ λαὸν κατεσκευασμένον. ¹⁸ Καὶ εἶπεν Ζαχαρίας πρὸς τὸν ἄγγελον, Κατὰ τί γνώσομαι τοῦτο; ἐγὼ γάρ εἰμι πρεσβύτης καὶ ἡ γυνή μου προβεβηκυῖα ἐν ταῖς ἡμέραις αὐτῆς. ¹⁹ καὶ ἀποκριθεὶς ὁ ἄγγελος εἶπεν αὐτῷ, Ἐγώ εἰμι Γαβριὴλ ὁ παρεστηκὼς ἐνώπιον τοῦ θεοῦ, καὶ ἀπεστάλην λαλῆσαι πρὸς σὲ καὶ εὐαγγελίσασθαί σοι ταῦτα· ²⁰ καὶ ἰδοὺ ἔσῃ σιωπῶν καὶ μὴ δυνάμενος λαλῆσαι ἄχρι ἧς ἡμέρας γένηται ταῦτα, ἀνθ' ὧν οὐκ ἐπίστευσας τοῖς λόγοις μου, οἵτινες πληρωθήσονται εἰς τὸν καιρὸν αὐτῶν. ²¹ Καὶ ἦν ὁ λαὸς προσδοκῶν τὸν Ζαχαρίαν, καὶ ἐθαύμαζον ἐν τῷ χρονίζειν ἐν τῷ ναῷ αὐτόν. ²² ἐξελθὼν δὲ οὐκ ἐδύνατο λαλῆσαι αὐτοῖς, καὶ ἐπέγνωσαν ὅτι ὀπτασίαν ἑώρακεν ἐν τῷ ναῷ· καὶ αὐτὸς ἦν διανεύων αὐτοῖς, καὶ διέμενεν κωφός. ²³ καὶ ἐγένετο ὡς ἐπλήσθησαν αἱ ἡμέραι τῆς λειτουργίας αὐτοῦ ἀπῆλθεν εἰς τὸν οἶκον αὐτοῦ. ²⁴ Μετὰ δὲ ταύτας τὰς ἡμέρας συνέλαβεν Ἐλισάβετ ἡ γυνὴ αὐτοῦ· καὶ περιέκρυβεν ἑαυτὴν μῆνας πέντε, λέγουσα ²⁵ ὅτι Οὕτως μοι πεποίηκεν κύριος ἐν ἡμέραις αἷς ἐπεῖδεν ἀφελεῖν ὄνειδός μου ἐν ἀνθρώποις.

English

⁵ In the days of King Herod of Judea, there was a priest named Zechariah, who belonged to the priestly order of Abijah. His wife was a descendant of Aaron, and her name was Elizabeth. ⁶ Both of them were righteous before God, living blamelessly according to all the commandments and regulations of the Lord. ⁷ But they had no children, because Elizabeth

was barren, and both were getting on in years. ⁸ Once when he was serving as priest before God and his section was on duty, ⁹ he was chosen by lot, according to the custom of the priesthood, to enter the sanctuary of the Lord and offer incense. ¹⁰ Now at the time of the incense offering, the whole assembly of the people was praying outside. ¹¹ Then there appeared to him an angel of the Lord, standing at the right side of the altar of incense. ¹² When Zechariah saw him, he was terrified; and fear overwhelmed him. ¹³ But the angel said to him, "Do not be afraid, Zechariah, for your prayer has been heard. Your wife Elizabeth will bear you a son, and you will name him John. ¹⁴ You will have joy and gladness, and many will rejoice at his birth, ¹⁵ for he will be great in the sight of the Lord. He must never drink wine or strong drink; even before his birth he will be filled with the Holy Spirit. ¹⁶ He will turn many of the people of Israel to the Lord their God. ¹⁷ With the spirit and power of Elijah he will go before him, to turn the hearts of parents to their children, and the disobedient to the wisdom of the righteous, to make ready a people prepared for the Lord." ¹⁸ Zechariah said to the angel, "How will I know that this is so? For I am an old man, and my wife is getting on in years." ¹⁹ The angel replied, "I am Gabriel. I stand in the presence of God, and I have been sent to speak to you and to bring you this good news. ²⁰ But now, because you did not believe my words, which will be fulfilled in their time, you will become mute, unable to speak, until the day these things occur." ²¹ Meanwhile the people were waiting for Zechariah, and wondered at his delay in the sanctuary. ²² When he did come out, he could not speak to them, and they realized that he had seen a vision in the sanctuary. He kept motioning to them and remained unable to speak. ²³ When his time of service was ended, he went to his home. ²⁴ After those days his wife Elizabeth conceived, and for five months she remained in seclusion. She said, ²⁵ "This is what the Lord has done for me when he looked favorably on me and took away the disgrace I have endured among my people."

BIRTH OF JESUS FORETOLD (1:26–38)

Greek

²⁶ Ἐν δὲ τῷ μηνὶ τῷ ἕκτῳ ἀπεστάλη ὁ ἄγγελος Γαβριὴλ ἀπὸ τοῦ θεοῦ εἰς πόλιν τῆς Γαλιλαίας ᾗ ὄνομα Ναζαρὲθ ²⁷ πρὸς παρθένον ἐμνηστευμένην ἀνδρὶ ᾧ ὄνομα Ἰωσὴφ ἐξ οἴκου Δαυίδ, καὶ τὸ ὄνομα τῆς παρθένου Μαριάμ.

²⁸ καὶ εἰσελθὼν πρὸς αὐτὴν εἶπεν, Χαῖρε, κεχαριτωμένη, ὁ κύριος μετὰ σοῦ. ²⁹ ἡ δὲ ἐπὶ τῷ λόγῳ διεταράχθη καὶ διελογίζετο ποταπὸς εἴη ὁ ἀσπασμὸς οὗτος. ³⁰ καὶ εἶπεν ὁ ἄγγελος αὐτῇ, Μὴ φοβοῦ, Μαριάμ, εὗρες γὰρ χάριν παρὰ τῷ θεῷ· ³¹ καὶ ἰδοὺ συλλήμψῃ ἐν γαστρὶ καὶ τέξῃ υἱόν, καὶ καλέσεις τὸ ὄνομα αὐτοῦ Ἰησοῦν. ³² οὗτος ἔσται μέγας καὶ υἱὸς ὑψίστου κληθήσεται, καὶ δώσει αὐτῷ κύριος ὁ θεὸς τὸν θρόνον Δαυὶδ τοῦ πατρὸς αὐτοῦ, ³³ καὶ βασιλεύσει ἐπὶ τὸν οἶκον Ἰακὼβ εἰς τοὺς αἰῶνας, καὶ τῆς βασιλείας αὐτοῦ οὐκ ἔσται τέλος. ³⁴ εἶπεν δὲ Μαριὰμ πρὸς τὸν ἄγγελον, Πῶς ἔσται τοῦτο, ἐπεὶ ἄνδρα οὐ γινώσκω; ³⁵ καὶ ἀποκριθεὶς ὁ ἄγγελος εἶπεν αὐτῇ, Πνεῦμα ἅγιον ἐπελεύσεται ἐπὶ σέ, καὶ δύναμις ὑψίστου ἐπισκιάσει σοι· διὸ καὶ τὸ γεννώμενον ἅγιον κληθήσεται, υἱὸς θεοῦ. ³⁶ καὶ ἰδοὺ Ἐλισάβετ ἡ συγγενίς σου καὶ αὐτὴ συνείληφεν υἱὸν ἐν γήρει αὐτῆς, καὶ οὗτος μὴν ἕκτος ἐστὶν αὐτῇ τῇ καλουμένῃ στείρᾳ· ³⁷ ὅτι οὐκ ἀδυνατήσει παρὰ τοῦ θεοῦ πᾶν ῥῆμα. ³⁸ εἶπεν δὲ Μαριάμ, Ἰδοὺ ἡ δούλη κυρίου· γένοιτό μοι κατὰ τὸ ῥῆμά σου. καὶ ἀπῆλθεν ἀπ᾽ αὐτῆς ὁ ἄγγελος.

English

²⁶ In the sixth month the angel Gabriel was sent by God to a town in Galilee called Nazareth, ²⁷ to a virgin engaged to a man whose name was Joseph, of the house of David. The virgin's name was Mary. ²⁸ And he came to her and said, "Greetings, favored one! The Lord is with you." ²⁹ But she was much perplexed by his words and pondered what sort of greeting this might be. ³⁰ The angel said to her, "Do not be afraid, Mary, for you have found favor with God. ³¹ And now, you will conceive in your womb and bear a son, and you will name him Jesus. ³² He will be great, and will be called the Son of the Most High, and the Lord God will give to him the throne of his ancestor David. ³³ He will reign over the house of Jacob forever, and of his kingdom there will be no end." ³⁴ Mary said to the angel, "How can this be, since I am a virgin?" ³⁵ The angel said to her, "The Holy Spirit will come upon you, and the power of the Most High will overshadow you; therefore the child to be born will be holy; he will be called Son of God. ³⁶ And now, your relative Elizabeth in her old age has also conceived a son; and this is the sixth month for her who was said to be barren. ³⁷ For nothing will be impossible with God." ³⁸ Then Mary said, "Here am I, the servant of the Lord; let it be with me according to your word." Then the angel departed from her.

MARY VISITS ELIZABETH (1:39–56)

Greek

³⁹ Ἀναστᾶσα δὲ Μαριὰμ ἐν ταῖς ἡμέραις ταύταις ἐπορεύθη εἰς τὴν ὀρεινὴν μετὰ σπουδῆς εἰς πόλιν Ἰούδα, ⁴⁰ καὶ εἰσῆλθεν εἰς τὸν οἶκον Ζαχαρίου καὶ ἠσπάσατο τὴν Ἐλισάβετ. ⁴¹ καὶ ἐγένετο ὡς ἤκουσεν τὸν ἀσπασμὸν τῆς Μαρίας ἡ Ἐλισάβετ, ἐσκίρτησεν τὸ βρέφος ἐν τῇ κοιλίᾳ αὐτῆς, καὶ ἐπλήσθη πνεύματος ἁγίου ἡ Ἐλισάβετ, ⁴² καὶ ἀνεφώνησεν κραυγῇ μεγάλῃ καὶ εἶπεν, Εὐλογημένη σὺ ἐν γυναιξίν, καὶ εὐλογημένος ὁ καρπὸς τῆς κοιλίας σου. ⁴³ καὶ πόθεν μοι τοῦτο ἵνα ἔλθῃ ἡ μήτηρ τοῦ κυρίου μου πρὸς ἐμέ; ⁴⁴ ἰδοὺ γὰρ ὡς ἐγένετο ἡ φωνὴ τοῦ ἀσπασμοῦ σου εἰς τὰ ὦτά μου, ἐσκίρτησεν ἐν ἀγαλλιάσει τὸ βρέφος ἐν τῇ κοιλίᾳ μου. ⁴⁵ καὶ μακαρία ἡ πιστεύσασα ὅτι ἔσται τελείωσις τοῖς λελαλημένοις αὐτῇ παρὰ κυρίου. ⁴⁶ Καὶ εἶπεν Μαριάμ, Μεγαλύνει ἡ ψυχή μου τὸν κύριον, ⁴⁷ καὶ ἠγαλλίασεν τὸ πνεῦμά μου ἐπὶ τῷ θεῷ τῷ σωτῆρί μου, ⁴⁸ ὅτι ἐπέβλεψεν ἐπὶ τὴν ταπείνωσιν τῆς δούλης αὐτοῦ. ἰδοὺ γὰρ ἀπὸ τοῦ νῦν μακαριοῦσίν με πᾶσαι αἱ γενεαί· ⁴⁹ ὅτι ἐποίησέν μοι μεγάλα ὁ δυνατός, καὶ ἅγιον τὸ ὄνομα αὐτοῦ, ⁵⁰ καὶ τὸ ἔλεος αὐτοῦ εἰς γενεὰς καὶ γενεὰς τοῖς φοβουμένοις αὐτόν. ⁵¹ Ἐποίησεν κράτος ἐν βραχίονι αὐτοῦ, διεσκόρπισεν ὑπερηφάνους διανοίᾳ καρδίας αὐτῶν· ⁵² καθεῖλεν δυνάστας ἀπὸ θρόνων καὶ ὕψωσεν ταπεινούς, ⁵³ πεινῶντας ἐνέπλησεν ἀγαθῶν καὶ πλουτοῦντας ἐξαπέστειλεν κενούς. ⁵⁴ ἀντελάβετο Ἰσραὴλ παιδὸς αὐτοῦ, μνησθῆναι ἐλέους, ⁵⁵ καθὼς ἐλάλησεν πρὸς τοὺς πατέρας ἡμῶν, τῷ Ἀβραὰμ καὶ τῷ σπέρματι αὐτοῦ εἰς τὸν αἰῶνα. ⁵⁶ Ἔμεινεν δὲ Μαριὰμ σὺν αὐτῇ ὡς μῆνας τρεῖς, καὶ ὑπέστρεψεν εἰς τὸν οἶκον αὐτῆς.

English

³⁹ In those days Mary set out and went with haste to a Judean town in the hill country, ⁴⁰ where she entered the house of Zechariah and greeted Elizabeth. ⁴¹ When Elizabeth heard Mary's greeting, the child leaped in her womb. And Elizabeth was filled with the Holy Spirit ⁴² and exclaimed with a loud cry, "Blessed are you among women, and blessed is the fruit of your womb. ⁴³ And why has this happened to me, that the mother of my Lord comes to me? ⁴⁴ For as soon as I heard the sound of your greeting, the child in my womb leaped for joy. ⁴⁵ And blessed is she who believed that there would be a fulfillment of what was spoken to her by the Lord." ⁴⁶ And Mary said, "My soul magnifies the Lord, ⁴⁷ and my

spirit rejoices in God my Savior, [48] for he has looked with favor on the lowliness of his servant. Surely, from now on all generations will call me blessed; [49] for the Mighty One has done great things for me, and holy is his name. [50] His mercy is for those who fear him from generation to generation. [51] He has shown strength with his arm; he has scattered the proud in the thoughts of their hearts. [52] He has brought down the powerful from their thrones, and lifted up the lowly; [53] he has filled the hungry with good things, and sent the rich away empty. [54] He has helped his servant Israel, in remembrance of his mercy, [55] according to the promise he made to our ancestors, to Abraham and to his descendants forever." [56] And Mary remained with her about three months and then returned to her home.

BIRTH OF JOHN THE BAPTIST (1:57–80)

Greek

[57] Τῇ δὲ Ἐλισάβετ ἐπλήσθη ὁ χρόνος τοῦ τεκεῖν αὐτήν, καὶ ἐγέννησεν υἱόν. [58] καὶ ἤκουσαν οἱ περίοικοι καὶ οἱ συγγενεῖς αὐτῆς ὅτι ἐμεγάλυνεν κύριος τὸ ἔλεος αὐτοῦ μετ᾽ αὐτῆς, καὶ συνέχαιρον αὐτῇ. [59] Καὶ ἐγένετο ἐν τῇ ἡμέρᾳ τῇ ὀγδόῃ ἦλθον περιτεμεῖν τὸ παιδίον, καὶ ἐκάλουν αὐτὸ ἐπὶ τῷ ὀνόματι τοῦ πατρὸς αὐτοῦ Ζαχαρίαν. [60] καὶ ἀποκριθεῖσα ἡ μήτηρ αὐτοῦ εἶπεν, Οὐχί, ἀλλὰ κληθήσεται Ἰωάννης. [61] καὶ εἶπαν πρὸς αὐτὴν ὅτι Οὐδείς ἐστιν ἐκ τῆς συγγενείας σου ὃς καλεῖται τῷ ὀνόματι τούτῳ. [62] ἐνένευον δὲ τῷ πατρὶ αὐτοῦ τὸ τί ἂν θέλοι καλεῖσθαι αὐτό. [63] καὶ αἰτήσας πινακίδιον ἔγραψεν λέγων, Ἰωάννης ἐστὶν ὄνομα αὐτοῦ. καὶ ἐθαύμασαν πάντες. [64] ἀνεῴχθη δὲ τὸ στόμα αὐτοῦ παραχρῆμα καὶ ἡ γλῶσσα αὐτοῦ, καὶ ἐλάλει εὐλογῶν τὸν θεόν. [65] καὶ ἐγένετο ἐπὶ πάντας φόβος τοὺς περιοικοῦντας αὐτούς, καὶ ἐν ὅλῃ τῇ ὀρεινῇ τῆς Ἰουδαίας διελαλεῖτο πάντα τὰ ῥήματα ταῦτα, [66] καὶ ἔθεντο πάντες οἱ ἀκούσαντες ἐν τῇ καρδίᾳ αὐτῶν, λέγοντες, Τί ἄρα τὸ παιδίον τοῦτο ἔσται; καὶ γὰρ χεὶρ κυρίου ἦν μετ᾽ αὐτοῦ. [67] Καὶ Ζαχαρίας ὁ πατὴρ αὐτοῦ ἐπλήσθη πνεύματος ἁγίου καὶ ἐπροφήτευσεν λέγων, [68] Εὐλογητὸς κύριος ὁ θεὸς τοῦ Ἰσραήλ, ὅτι ἐπεσκέψατο καὶ ἐποίησεν λύτρωσιν τῷ λαῷ αὐτοῦ, [69] καὶ ἤγειρεν κέρας σωτηρίας ἡμῖν ἐν οἴκῳ Δαυὶδ παιδὸς αὐτοῦ, [70] καθὼς ἐλάλησεν διὰ στόματος τῶν ἁγίων ἀπ᾽ αἰῶνος προφητῶν αὐτοῦ, [71] σωτηρίαν ἐξ ἐχθρῶν ἡμῶν καὶ ἐκ χειρὸς πάντων τῶν μισούντων ἡμᾶς· [72] ποιῆσαι ἔλεος μετὰ τῶν πατέρων ἡμῶν καὶ μνησθῆναι διαθήκης ἁγίας αὐτοῦ, [73] ὅρκον ὃν ὤμοσεν πρὸς Ἀβραὰμ τὸν πατέρα ἡμῶν, τοῦ δοῦναι

ἡμῖν ⁷⁴ ἀφόβως ἐκ χειρὸς ἐχθρῶν ῥυσθέντας λατρεύειν αὐτῷ ⁷⁵ ἐν ὁσιότητι
καὶ δικαιοσύνῃ ἐνώπιον αὐτοῦ πάσαις ταῖς ἡμέραις ἡμῶν. ⁷⁶ Καὶ σὺ δέ,
παιδίον, προφήτης ὑψίστου κληθήσῃ, προπορεύσῃ γὰρ ἐνώπιον κυρίου
ἑτοιμάσαι ὁδοὺς αὐτοῦ, ⁷⁷ τοῦ δοῦναι γνῶσιν σωτηρίας τῷ λαῷ αὐτοῦ
ἐν ἀφέσει ἁμαρτιῶν αὐτῶν, ⁷⁸ διὰ σπλάγχνα ἐλέους θεοῦ ἡμῶν, ἐν οἷς
ἐπισκέψεται ἡμᾶς ἀνατολὴ ἐξ ὕψους, ⁷⁹ ἐπιφᾶναι τοῖς ἐν σκότει καὶ σκιᾷ
θανάτου καθημένοις, τοῦ κατευθῦναι τοὺς πόδας ἡμῶν εἰς ὁδὸν εἰρήνης. ⁸⁰
Τὸ δὲ παιδίον ηὔξανεν καὶ ἐκραταιοῦτο πνεύματι, καὶ ἦν ἐν ταῖς ἐρήμοις
ἕως ἡμέρας ἀναδείξεως αὐτοῦ πρὸς τὸν Ἰσραήλ.

English

⁵⁷ Now the time came for Elizabeth to give birth, and she bore a son. ⁵⁸
Her neighbors and relatives heard that the Lord had shown his great
mercy to her, and they rejoiced with her. ⁵⁹ On the eighth day they came
to circumcise the child, and they were going to name him Zechariah
after his father. ⁶⁰ But his mother said, "No; he is to be called John." ⁶¹
They said to her, "None of your relatives has this name." ⁶² Then they
began motioning to his father to find out what name he wanted to give
him. ⁶³ He asked for a writing tablet and wrote, "His name is John." And
all of them were amazed. ⁶⁴ Immediately his mouth was opened and his
tongue freed, and he began to speak, praising God. ⁶⁵ Fear came over all
their neighbors, and all these things were talked about throughout the
entire hill country of Judea. ⁶⁶ All who heard them pondered them and
said, "What then will this child become?" For, indeed, the hand of the
Lord was with him. ⁶⁷ Then his father Zechariah was filled with the Holy
Spirit and spoke this prophecy: ⁶⁸ "Blessed be the Lord God of Israel,
for he has looked favorably on his people and redeemed them. ⁶⁹ He has
raised up a mighty savior for us in the house of his servant David, ⁷⁰ as
he spoke through the mouth of his holy prophets from of old, ⁷¹ that we
would be saved from our enemies and from the hand of all who hate
us. ⁷² Thus he has shown the mercy promised to our ancestors, and has
remembered his holy covenant, ⁷³ the oath that he swore to our ancestor
Abraham, to grant us ⁷⁴ that we, being rescued from the hands of our
enemies, might serve him without fear, ⁷⁵ in holiness and righteousness
before him all our days. ⁷⁶ And you, child, will be called the prophet of
the Most High; for you will go before the Lord to prepare his ways, ⁷⁷ to
give knowledge of salvation to his people by the forgiveness of their sins.
⁷⁸ By the tender mercy of our God, the dawn from on high will break

upon us, [79] to give light to those who sit in darkness and in the shadow of death, to guide our feet into the way of peace." [80] The child grew and became strong in spirit, and he was in the wilderness until the day he appeared publicly to Israel.

BIRTH OF JESUS (2:1–20)

Greek

[1] Ἐγένετο δὲ ἐν ταῖς ἡμέραις ἐκείναις ἐξῆλθεν δόγμα παρὰ Καίσαρος Αὐγούστου ἀπογράφεσθαι πᾶσαν τὴν οἰκουμένην. [2] αὕτη ἀπογραφὴ πρώτη ἐγένετο ἡγεμονεύοντος τῆς Συρίας Κυρηνίου. [3] καὶ ἐπορεύοντο πάντες ἀπογράφεσθαι, ἕκαστος εἰς τὴν ἑαυτοῦ πόλιν. [4] Ἀνέβη δὲ καὶ Ἰωσὴφ ἀπὸ τῆς Γαλιλαίας ἐκ πόλεως Ναζαρὲθ εἰς τὴν Ἰουδαίαν εἰς πόλιν Δαυὶδ ἥτις καλεῖται Βηθλέεμ, διὰ τὸ εἶναι αὐτὸν ἐξ οἴκου καὶ πατριᾶς Δαυίδ, [5] ἀπογράψασθαι σὺν Μαριὰμ τῇ ἐμνηστευμένῃ αὐτῷ, οὔσῃ ἐγκύῳ. [6] ἐγένετο δὲ ἐν τῷ εἶναι αὐτοὺς ἐκεῖ ἐπλήσθησαν αἱ ἡμέραι τοῦ τεκεῖν αὐτήν, [7] καὶ ἔτεκεν τὸν υἱὸν αὐτῆς τὸν πρωτότοκον· καὶ ἐσπαργάνωσεν αὐτὸν καὶ ἀνέκλινεν αὐτὸν ἐν φάτνῃ, διότι οὐκ ἦν αὐτοῖς τόπος ἐν τῷ καταλύματι. [8] Καὶ ποιμένες ἦσαν ἐν τῇ χώρᾳ τῇ αὐτῇ ἀγραυλοῦντες καὶ φυλάσσοντες φυλακὰς τῆς νυκτὸς ἐπὶ τὴν ποίμνην αὐτῶν. [9] καὶ ἄγγελος κυρίου ἐπέστη αὐτοῖς καὶ δόξα κυρίου περιέλαμψεν αὐτούς, καὶ ἐφοβήθησαν φόβον μέγαν. [10] καὶ εἶπεν αὐτοῖς ὁ ἄγγελος, Μὴ φοβεῖσθε, ἰδοὺ γὰρ εὐαγγελίζομαι ὑμῖν χαρὰν μεγάλην ἥτις ἔσται παντὶ τῷ λαῷ, [11] ὅτι ἐτέχθη ὑμῖν σήμερον σωτὴρ ὅς ἐστιν Χριστὸς κύριος ἐν πόλει Δαυίδ· [12] καὶ τοῦτο ὑμῖν τὸ σημεῖον, εὑρήσετε βρέφος ἐσπαργανωμένον καὶ κείμενον ἐν φάτνῃ. [13] καὶ ἐξαίφνης ἐγένετο σὺν τῷ ἀγγέλῳ πλῆθος στρατιᾶς οὐρανίου αἰνούντων τὸν θεὸν καὶ λεγόντων, [14] Δόξα ἐν ὑψίστοις θεῷ καὶ ἐπὶ γῆς εἰρήνη ἐν ἀνθρώποις εὐδοκίας. [15] Καὶ ἐγένετο ὡς ἀπῆλθον ἀπ' αὐτῶν εἰς τὸν οὐρανὸν οἱ ἄγγελοι, οἱ ποιμένες ἐλάλουν πρὸς ἀλλήλους, Διέλθωμεν δὴ ἕως Βηθλέεμ καὶ ἴδωμεν τὸ ῥῆμα τοῦτο τὸ γεγονὸς ὃ ὁ κύριος ἐγνώρισεν ἡμῖν. [16] καὶ ἦλθον σπεύσαντες καὶ ἀνεῦρον τήν τε Μαριὰμ καὶ τὸν Ἰωσὴφ καὶ τὸ βρέφος κείμενον ἐν τῇ φάτνῃ· [17] ἰδόντες δὲ ἐγνώρισαν περὶ τοῦ ῥήματος τοῦ λαληθέντος αὐτοῖς περὶ τοῦ παιδίου τούτου. [18] καὶ πάντες οἱ ἀκούσαντες ἐθαύμασαν περὶ τῶν λαληθέντων ὑπὸ τῶν ποιμένων πρὸς αὐτούς· [19] ἡ δὲ Μαριὰμ πάντα συνετήρει τὰ ῥήματα ταῦτα συμβάλλουσα ἐν τῇ καρδίᾳ αὐτῆς. [20] καὶ ὑπέστρεψαν οἱ ποιμένες δοξάζοντες καὶ αἰνοῦντες τὸν θεὸν ἐπὶ πᾶσιν οἷς ἤκουσαν καὶ εἶδον καθὼς ἐλαλήθη πρὸς αὐτούς.

English

¹ In those days a decree went out from Emperor Augustus that all the world should be registered. ² This was the first registration and was taken while Quirinius was governor of Syria. ³ All went to their own towns to be registered. ⁴ Joseph also went from the town of Nazareth in Galilee to Judea, to the city of David called Bethlehem, because he was descended from the house and family of David. ⁵ He went to be registered with Mary, to whom he was engaged and who was expecting a child. ⁶ While they were there, the time came for her to deliver her child. ⁷ And she gave birth to her firstborn son and wrapped him in bands of cloth, and laid him in a manger, because there was no place for them in the inn. ⁸ In that region there were shepherds living in the fields, keeping watch over their flock by night. ⁹ Then an angel of the Lord stood before them, and the glory of the Lord shone around them, and they were terrified. ¹⁰ But the angel said to them, "Do not be afraid; for see—I am bringing you good news of great joy for all the people: ¹¹ to you is born this day in the city of David a Savior, who is the Messiah, the Lord. ¹² This will be a sign for you: you will find a child wrapped in bands of cloth and lying in a manger." ¹³ And suddenly there was with the angel a multitude of the heavenly host, praising God and saying, ¹⁴ "Glory to God in the highest heaven, and on earth peace among those whom he favors!" ¹⁵ When the angels had left them and gone into heaven, the shepherds said to one another, "Let us go now to Bethlehem and see this thing that has taken place, which the Lord has made known to us." ¹⁶ So they went with haste and found Mary and Joseph, and the child lying in the manger. ¹⁷ When they saw this, they made known what had been told them about this child; ¹⁸ and all who heard it were amazed at what the shepherds told them. ¹⁹ But Mary treasured all these words and pondered them in her heart. ²⁰ The shepherds returned, glorifying and praising God for all they had heard and seen, as it had been told them.

JESUS IS PRESENTED IN THE TEMPLE (2:21–38)

Greek

²¹ Καὶ ὅτε ἐπλήσθησαν ἡμέραι ὀκτὼ τοῦ περιτεμεῖν αὐτόν, καὶ ἐκλήθη τὸ ὄνομα αὐτοῦ Ἰησοῦς, τὸ κληθὲν ὑπὸ τοῦ ἀγγέλου πρὸ τοῦ συλλημφθῆναι αὐτὸν ἐν τῇ κοιλίᾳ. ²² Καὶ ὅτε ἐπλήσθησαν αἱ ἡμέραι τοῦ καθαρισμοῦ αὐτῶν κατὰ τὸν νόμον Μωϋσέως, ἀνήγαγον αὐτὸν εἰς Ἱεροσόλυμα παραστῆσαι

τῷ κυρίῳ, ²³ καθὼς γέγραπται ἐν νόμῳ κυρίου ὅτι Πᾶν ἄρσεν διανοῖγον μήτραν ἅγιον τῷ κυρίῳ κληθήσεται, ²⁴ καὶ τοῦ δοῦναι θυσίαν κατὰ τὸ εἰρημένον ἐν τῷ νόμῳ κυρίου, ζεῦγος τρυγόνων ἢ δύο νοσσοὺς περιστερῶν. ²⁵ Καὶ ἰδοὺ ἄνθρωπος ἦν ἐν Ἰερουσαλὴμ ᾧ ὄνομα Συμεών, καὶ ὁ ἄνθρωπος οὗτος δίκαιος καὶ εὐλαβής, προσδεχόμενος παράκλησιν τοῦ Ἰσραήλ, καὶ πνεῦμα ἦν ἅγιον ἐπ᾽ αὐτόν· ²⁶ καὶ ἦν αὐτῷ κεχρηματισμένον ὑπὸ τοῦ πνεύματος τοῦ ἁγίου μὴ ἰδεῖν θάνατον πρὶν [ἢ] ἂν ἴδῃ τὸν Χριστὸν κυρίου. ²⁷ καὶ ἦλθεν ἐν τῷ πνεύματι εἰς τὸ ἱερόν· καὶ ἐν τῷ εἰσαγαγεῖν τοὺς γονεῖς τὸ παιδίον Ἰησοῦν τοῦ ποιῆσαι αὐτοὺς κατὰ τὸ εἰθισμένον τοῦ νόμου περὶ αὐτοῦ ²⁸ καὶ αὐτὸς ἐδέξατο αὐτὸ εἰς τὰς ἀγκάλας καὶ εὐλόγησεν τὸν θεὸν καὶ εἶπεν, ²⁹ Νῦν ἀπολύεις τὸν δοῦλόν σου, δέσποτα, κατὰ τὸ ῥῆμά σου ἐν εἰρήνῃ· ³⁰ ὅτι εἶδον οἱ ὀφθαλμοί μου τὸ σωτήριόν σου ³¹ ὃ ἡτοίμασας κατὰ πρόσωπον πάντων τῶν λαῶν, ³² φῶς εἰς ἀποκάλυψιν ἐθνῶν καὶ δόξαν λαοῦ σου Ἰσραήλ. ³³ καὶ ἦν ὁ πατὴρ αὐτοῦ καὶ ἡ μήτηρ θαυμάζοντες ἐπὶ τοῖς λαλουμένοις περὶ αὐτοῦ. ³⁴ καὶ εὐλόγησεν αὐτοὺς Συμεὼν καὶ εἶπεν πρὸς Μαριὰμ τὴν μητέρα αὐτοῦ, Ἰδοὺ οὗτος κεῖται εἰς πτῶσιν καὶ ἀνάστασιν πολλῶν ἐν τῷ Ἰσραὴλ καὶ εἰς σημεῖον ἀντιλεγόμενον ³⁵ [καὶ σοῦ [δὲ] αὐτῆς τὴν ψυχὴν διελεύσεται ῥομφαία], ὅπως ἂν ἀποκαλυφθῶσιν ἐκ πολλῶν καρδιῶν διαλογισμοί. ³⁶ Καὶ ἦν Ἅννα προφῆτις, θυγάτηρ Φανουήλ, ἐκ φυλῆς Ἀσήρ· αὕτη προβεβηκυῖα ἐν ἡμέραις πολλαῖς, ζήσασα μετὰ ἀνδρὸς ἔτη ἑπτὰ ἀπὸ τῆς παρθενίας αὐτῆς, ³⁷ καὶ αὐτὴ χήρα ἕως ἐτῶν ὀγδοήκοντα τεσσάρων, ἣ οὐκ ἀφίστατο τοῦ ἱεροῦ νηστείαις καὶ δεήσεσιν λατρεύουσα νύκτα καὶ ἡμέραν. ³⁸ καὶ αὐτῇ τῇ ὥρᾳ ἐπιστᾶσα ἀνθωμολογεῖτο τῷ θεῷ καὶ ἐλάλει περὶ αὐτοῦ πᾶσιν τοῖς προσδεχομένοις λύτρωσιν Ἰερουσαλήμ.

English

²¹ After eight days had passed, it was time to circumcise the child; and he was called Jesus, the name given by the angel before he was conceived in the womb. ²² When the time came for their purification according to the law of Moses, they brought him up to Jerusalem to present him to the Lord ²³ (as it is written in the law of the Lord, "Every firstborn male shall be designated as holy to the Lord"), ²⁴ and they offered a sacrifice according to what is stated in the law of the Lord, "a pair of turtledoves or two young pigeons." ²⁵ Now there was a man in Jerusalem whose name was Simeon; this man was righteous and devout, looking forward to the consolation of Israel, and the Holy Spirit rested on him. ²⁶ It had been revealed to him by the Holy Spirit that he would not see death before he had seen the Lord's Messiah. ²⁷ Guided by the Spirit, Simeon came

into the temple; and when the parents brought in the child Jesus, to do for him what was customary under the law, ²⁸ Simeon took him in his arms and praised God, saying, ²⁹ "Master, now you are dismissing your servant in peace, according to your word; ³⁰ for my eyes have seen your salvation, ³¹ which you have prepared in the presence of all peoples, ³² a light for revelation to the Gentiles and for glory to your people Israel." ³³ And the child's father and mother were amazed at what was being said about him. ³⁴ Then Simeon blessed them and said to his mother Mary, "This child is destined for the falling and the rising of many in Israel, and to be a sign that will be opposed ³⁵ so that the inner thoughts of many will be revealed—and a sword will pierce your own soul too." ³⁶ There was also a prophet, Anna the daughter of Phanuel, of the tribe of Asher. She was of a great age, having lived with her husband seven years after her marriage, ³⁷ then as a widow to the age of eighty-four. She never left the temple but worshiped there with fasting and prayer night and day. ³⁸ At that moment she came, and began to praise God and to speak about the child to all who were looking for the redemption of Jerusalem.

THE BOY JESUS IN THE TEMPLE (2:41–52)

Greek

⁴¹ Καὶ ἐπορεύοντο οἱ γονεῖς αὐτοῦ κατ' ἔτος εἰς Ἰερουσαλὴμ τῇ ἑορτῇ τοῦ πάσχα. ⁴² καὶ ὅτε ἐγένετο ἐτῶν δώδεκα, ἀναβαινόντων αὐτῶν κατὰ τὸ ἔθος τῆς ἑορτῆς ⁴³ καὶ τελειωσάντων τὰς ἡμέρας, ἐν τῷ ὑποστρέφειν αὐτοὺς ὑπέμεινεν Ἰησοῦς ὁ παῖς ἐν Ἰερουσαλήμ, καὶ οὐκ ἔγνωσαν οἱ γονεῖς αὐτοῦ. ⁴⁴ νομίσαντες δὲ αὐτὸν εἶναι ἐν τῇ συνοδίᾳ ἦλθον ἡμέρας ὁδὸν καὶ ἀνεζήτουν αὐτὸν ἐν τοῖς συγγενεῦσιν καὶ τοῖς γνωστοῖς, ⁴⁵ καὶ μὴ εὑρόντες ὑπέστρεψαν εἰς Ἰερουσαλὴμ ἀναζητοῦντες αὐτόν. ⁴⁶ καὶ ἐγένετο μετὰ ἡμέρας τρεῖς εὗρον αὐτὸν ἐν τῷ ἱερῷ καθεζόμενον ἐν μέσῳ τῶν διδασκάλων καὶ ἀκούοντα αὐτῶν καὶ ἐπερωτῶντα αὐτούς· ⁴⁷ ἐξίσταντο δὲ πάντες οἱ ἀκούοντες αὐτοῦ ἐπὶ τῇ συνέσει καὶ ταῖς ἀποκρίσεσιν αὐτοῦ. ⁴⁸ καὶ ἰδόντες αὐτὸν ἐξεπλάγησαν, καὶ εἶπεν πρὸς αὐτὸν ἡ μήτηρ αὐτοῦ, Τέκνον, τί ἐποίησας ἡμῖν οὕτως; ἰδοὺ ὁ πατήρ σου κἀγὼ ὀδυνώμενοι ἐζητοῦμέν σε. ⁴⁹ καὶ εἶπεν πρὸς αὐτούς, Τί ὅτι ἐζητεῖτέ με; οὐκ ᾔδειτε ὅτι ἐν τοῖς τοῦ πατρός μου δεῖ εἶναί με; ⁵⁰ καὶ αὐτοὶ οὐ συνῆκαν τὸ ῥῆμα ὃ ἐλάλησεν αὐτοῖς. ⁵¹ καὶ κατέβη μετ' αὐτῶν καὶ ἦλθεν εἰς Ναζαρέθ, καὶ ἦν ὑποτασσόμενος αὐτοῖς. καὶ ἡ μήτηρ αὐτοῦ διετήρει πάντα τὰ ῥήματα ἐν τῇ καρδίᾳ αὐτῆς. ⁵² Καὶ Ἰησοῦς προέκοπτεν [ἐν τῇ] σοφίᾳ καὶ ἡλικίᾳ καὶ χάριτι παρὰ θεῷ καὶ ἀνθρώποις.

English

⁴¹ Now every year his parents went to Jerusalem for the festival of the Passover. ⁴² And when he was twelve years old, they went up as usual for the festival. ⁴³ When the festival was ended and they started to return, the boy Jesus stayed behind in Jerusalem, but his parents did not know it. ⁴⁴ Assuming that he was in the group of travelers, they went a day's journey. Then they started to look for him among their relatives and friends. ⁴⁵ When they did not find him, they returned to Jerusalem to search for him. ⁴⁶ After three days they found him in the temple, sitting among the teachers, listening to them and asking them questions. ⁴⁷ And all who heard him were amazed at his understanding and his answers. ⁴⁸ When his parents saw him they were astonished; and his mother said to him, "Child, why have you treated us like this? Look, your father and I have been searching for you in great anxiety." ⁴⁹ He said to them, "Why were you searching for me? Did you not know that I must be in my Father's house?" ⁵⁰ But they did not understand what he said to them. ⁵¹ Then he went down with them and came to Nazareth, and was obedient to them. His mother treasured all these things in her heart. ⁵² And Jesus increased in wisdom and in years, and in divine and human favor.

JOHN REPLIES TO QUESTIONS (3:10-14)

Greek

¹⁰ Καὶ ἐπηρώτων αὐτὸν οἱ ὄχλοι λέγοντες, Τί οὖν ποιήσωμεν; ¹¹ ἀποκριθεὶς δὲ ἔλεγεν αὐτοῖς, Ὁ ἔχων δύο χιτῶνας μεταδότω τῷ μὴ ἔχοντι, καὶ ὁ ἔχων βρώματα ὁμοίως ποιείτω. ¹² ἦλθον δὲ καὶ τελῶναι βαπτισθῆναι καὶ εἶπαν πρὸς αὐτόν, Διδάσκαλε, τί ποιήσωμεν; ¹³ ὁ δὲ εἶπεν πρὸς αὐτούς, Μηδὲν πλέον παρὰ τὸ διατεταγμένον ὑμῖν πράσσετε. ¹⁴ ἐπηρώτων δὲ αὐτὸν καὶ στρατευόμενοι λέγοντες, Τί ποιήσωμεν καὶ ἡμεῖς; καὶ εἶπεν αὐτοῖς, Μηδένα διασείσητε μηδὲ συκοφαντήσητε, καὶ ἀρκεῖσθε τοῖς ὀψωνίοις ὑμῶν.

English

¹⁰ And the crowds asked him, "What then should we do?" ¹¹ In reply he said to them, "Whoever has two coats must share with anyone who has none; and whoever has food must do likewise." ¹² Even tax collectors came to be baptized, and they asked him, "Teacher, what should we do?" ¹³ He said to them, "Collect no more than the amount prescribed for

you." ¹⁴ Soldiers also asked him, "And we, what should we do?" He said to them, "Do not extort money from anyone by threats or false accusation, and be satisfied with your wages."

GENEALOGY OF JESUS (3:23–38)

Greek

²³ Καὶ αὐτὸς ἦν Ἰησοῦς ἀρχόμενος ὡσεὶ ἐτῶν τριάκοντα, ὢν υἱός, ὡς ἐνομίζετο, Ἰωσὴφ τοῦ Ἠλὶ ²⁴ τοῦ Ματθὰτ τοῦ Λευὶ τοῦ Μελχὶ τοῦ Ἰανναὶ τοῦ Ἰωσὴφ ²⁵ τοῦ Ματταθίου τοῦ Ἀμὼς τοῦ Ναοὺμ τοῦ Ἑσλὶ τοῦ Ναγγαὶ ²⁶ τοῦ Μάαθ τοῦ Ματταθίου τοῦ Σεμεῒν τοῦ Ἰωσὴχ τοῦ Ἰωδὰ ²⁷ τοῦ Ἰωανὰν τοῦ Ῥησὰ τοῦ Ζοροβαβὲλ τοῦ Σαλαθιὴλ τοῦ Νηρὶ ²⁸ τοῦ Μελχὶ τοῦ Ἀδδὶ τοῦ Κωσὰμ τοῦ Ἐλμαδὰμ τοῦ Ἢρ ²⁹ τοῦ Ἰησοῦ τοῦ Ἐλιέζερ τοῦ Ἰωρὶμ τοῦ Ματθὰτ τοῦ Λευὶ ³⁰ τοῦ Συμεὼν τοῦ Ἰούδα τοῦ Ἰωσὴφ τοῦ Ἰωνὰμ τοῦ Ἐλιακὶμ ³¹ τοῦ Μελεὰ τοῦ Μεννὰ τοῦ Ματταθὰ τοῦ Ναθὰμ τοῦ Δαυὶδ ³² τοῦ Ἰεσσαὶ τοῦ Ἰωβὴδ τοῦ Βόος τοῦ Σαλὰ τοῦ Ναασσὼν ³³ τοῦ Ἀμιναδὰβ τοῦ Ἀδμὶν τοῦ Ἀρνὶ τοῦ Ἑσρὼμ τοῦ Φάρες τοῦ Ἰούδα ³⁴ τοῦ Ἰακὼβ τοῦ Ἰσαὰκ τοῦ Ἀβραὰμ τοῦ Θάρα τοῦ Ναχὼρ ³⁵ τοῦ Σεροὺχ τοῦ Ῥαγαὺ τοῦ Φάλεκ τοῦ Ἔβερ τοῦ Σαλὰ ³⁶ τοῦ Καϊνὰμ τοῦ Ἀρφαξὰδ τοῦ Σὴμ τοῦ Νῶε τοῦ Λάμεχ ³⁷ τοῦ Μαθουσαλὰ τοῦ Ἑνὼχ τοῦ Ἰάρετ τοῦ Μαλελεὴλ τοῦ Καϊνὰμ ³⁸ τοῦ Ἐνὼς τοῦ Σὴθ τοῦ Ἀδὰμ τοῦ θεοῦ.

English

²³ Jesus was about thirty years old when he began his work. He was the son (as was thought) of Joseph son of Heli, ²⁴ son of Matthat, son of Levi, son of Melchi, son of Jannai, son of Joseph, ²⁵ son of Mattathias, son of Amos, son of Nahum, son of Esli, son of Naggai, ²⁶ son of Maath, son of Mattathias, son of Semein, son of Josech, son of Joda, ²⁷ son of Joanan, son of Rhesa, son of Zerubbabel, son of Shealtiel, son of Neri, ²⁸ son of Melchi, son of Addi, son of Cosam, son of Elmadam, son of Er, ²⁹ son of Joshua, son of Eliezer, son of Jorim, son of Matthat, son of Levi, ³⁰ son of Simeon, son of Judah, son of Joseph, son of Jonam, son of Eliakim, ³¹ son of Melea, son of Menna, son of Mattatha, son of Nathan, son of David, ³² son of Jesse, son of Obed, son of Boaz, son of Sala, son of Nahshon, ³³ son of Amminadab, son of Admin, son of Arni, son of Hezron, son of Perez, son of Judah, ³⁴ son of Jacob, son of Isaac, son of Abraham, son of Terah, son of Nahor, ³⁵ son of Serug, son of Reu, son of Peleg, son of

Eber, son of Shelah, [36] son of Cainan, son of Arphaxad, son of Shem, son of Noah, son of Lamech, [37] son of Methuselah, son of Enoch, son of Jared, son of Mahalaleel, son of Cainan, [38] son of Enos, son of Seth, son of Adam, son of God.

GOOD NEWS TO THE POOR (4:14–23, 25–30)

Greek

[14] Καὶ ὑπέστρεψεν ὁ Ἰησοῦς ἐν τῇ δυνάμει τοῦ πνεύματος εἰς τὴν Γαλιλαίαν. καὶ φήμη ἐξῆλθεν καθ᾽ ὅλης τῆς περιχώρου περὶ αὐτοῦ. [15] καὶ αὐτὸς ἐδίδασκεν ἐν ταῖς συναγωγαῖς αὐτῶν, δοξαζόμενος ὑπὸ πάντων. [16] Καὶ ἦλθεν εἰς Ναζαρά, οὗ ἦν τεθραμμένος, καὶ εἰσῆλθεν κατὰ τὸ εἰωθὸς αὐτῷ ἐν τῇ ἡμέρᾳ τῶν σαββάτων εἰς τὴν συναγωγήν, καὶ ἀνέστη ἀναγνῶναι. [17] καὶ ἐπεδόθη αὐτῷ βιβλίον τοῦ προφήτου Ἠσαΐου, καὶ ἀναπτύξας τὸ βιβλίον εὗρεν τὸν τόπον οὗ ἦν γεγραμμένον, [18] Πνεῦμα κυρίου ἐπ᾽ ἐμέ, οὗ εἵνεκεν ἔχρισέν με εὐαγγελίσασθαι πτωχοῖς, ἀπέσταλκέν με κηρύξαι αἰχμαλώτοις ἄφεσιν καὶ τυφλοῖς ἀνάβλεψιν, ἀποστεῖλαι τεθραυσμένους ἐν ἀφέσει, [19] κηρύξαι ἐνιαυτὸν κυρίου δεκτόν. [20] καὶ πτύξας τὸ βιβλίον ἀποδοὺς τῷ ὑπηρέτῃ ἐκάθισεν· καὶ πάντων οἱ ὀφθαλμοὶ ἐν τῇ συναγωγῇ ἦσαν ἀτενίζοντες αὐτῷ. [21] ἤρξατο δὲ λέγειν πρὸς αὐτοὺς ὅτι Σήμερον πεπλήρωται ἡ γραφὴ αὕτη ἐν τοῖς ὠσὶν ὑμῶν. [22] Καὶ πάντες ἐμαρτύρουν αὐτῷ καὶ ἐθαύμαζον ἐπὶ τοῖς λόγοις τῆς χάριτος τοῖς ἐκπορευομένοις ἐκ τοῦ στόματος αὐτοῦ, καὶ ἔλεγον, Οὐχὶ υἱός ἐστιν Ἰωσὴφ οὗτος; [23] καὶ εἶπεν πρὸς αὐτούς, Πάντως ἐρεῖτέ μοι τὴν παραβολὴν ταύτην· Ἰατρέ, θεράπευσον σεαυτόν· ὅσα ἠκούσαμεν γενόμενα εἰς τὴν Καφαρναοὺμ ποίησον καὶ ὧδε ἐν τῇ πατρίδι σου.

[25] ἐπ᾽ ἀληθείας δὲ λέγω ὑμῖν, πολλαὶ χῆραι ἦσαν ἐν ταῖς ἡμέραις Ἠλίου ἐν τῷ Ἰσραήλ, ὅτε ἐκλείσθη ὁ οὐρανὸς ἐπὶ ἔτη τρία καὶ μῆνας ἕξ, ὡς ἐγένετο λιμὸς μέγας ἐπὶ πᾶσαν τὴν γῆν, [26] καὶ πρὸς οὐδεμίαν αὐτῶν ἐπέμφθη Ἠλίας εἰ μὴ εἰς Σάρεπτα τῆς Σιδωνίας πρὸς γυναῖκα χήραν. [27] καὶ πολλοὶ λεπροὶ ἦσαν ἐν τῷ Ἰσραὴλ ἐπὶ Ἐλισαίου τοῦ προφήτου, καὶ οὐδεὶς αὐτῶν ἐκαθαρίσθη εἰ μὴ Ναιμὰν ὁ Σύρος. [28] καὶ ἐπλήσθησαν πάντες θυμοῦ ἐν τῇ συναγωγῇ ἀκούοντες ταῦτα, [29] καὶ ἀναστάντες ἐξέβαλον αὐτὸν ἔξω τῆς πόλεως, καὶ ἤγαγον αὐτὸν ἕως ὀφρύος τοῦ ὄρους ἐφ᾽ οὗ ἡ πόλις ᾠκοδόμητο αὐτῶν, ὥστε κατακρημνίσαι αὐτόν· [30] αὐτὸς δὲ διελθὼν διὰ μέσου αὐτῶν ἐπορεύετο.

English

¹⁴ Then Jesus, filled with the power of the Spirit, returned to Galilee, and a report about him spread through all the surrounding country. ¹⁵ He began to teach in their synagogues and was praised by everyone. ¹⁶ When he came to Nazareth, where he had been brought up, he went to the synagogue on the sabbath day, as was his custom. He stood up to read, ¹⁷ and the scroll of the prophet Isaiah was given to him. He unrolled the scroll and found the place where it was written: ¹⁸ "The Spirit of the Lord is upon me, because he has anointed me to bring good news to the poor. He has sent me to proclaim release to the captives and recovery of sight to the blind, to let the oppressed go free, ¹⁹ to proclaim the year of the Lord's favor." ²⁰ And he rolled up the scroll, gave it back to the attendant, and sat down. The eyes of all in the synagogue were fixed on him. ²¹ Then he began to say to them, "Today this scripture has been fulfilled in your hearing." ²² All spoke well of him and were amazed at the gracious words that came from his mouth. They said, "Is not this Joseph's son?" ²³ He said to them, "Doubtless you will quote to me this proverb, 'Doctor, cure yourself!' And you will say, 'Do here also in your hometown the things that we have heard you did at Capernaum.'"

²⁵ "But the truth is, there were many widows in Israel in the time of Elijah, when the heaven was shut up three years and six months, and there was a severe famine over all the land; ²⁶ yet Elijah was sent to none of them except to a widow at Zarephath in Sidon. ²⁷ There were also many lepers in Israel in the time of the prophet Elisha, and none of them was cleansed except Naaman the Syrian." ²⁸ When they heard this, all in the synagogue were filled with rage. ²⁹ They got up, drove him out of the town, and led him to the brow of the hill on which their town was built, so that they might hurl him off the cliff. ³⁰ But he passed through the midst of them and went on his way.

CALL OF FIRST DISCIPLES/CATCH OF FISH (5:1–11)

Greek

¹ Ἐγένετο δὲ ἐν τῷ τὸν ὄχλον ἐπικεῖσθαι αὐτῷ καὶ ἀκούειν τὸν λόγον τοῦ θεοῦ καὶ αὐτὸς ἦν ἑστὼς παρὰ τὴν λίμνην Γεννησαρέτ, ² καὶ εἶδεν δύο πλοῖα ἑστῶτα παρὰ τὴν λίμνην· οἱ δὲ ἁλιεῖς ἀπ᾽ αὐτῶν ἀποβάντες ἔπλυνον

τὰ δίκτυα. ³ ἐμβὰς δὲ εἰς ἓν τῶν πλοίων, ὃ ἦν Σίμωνος, ἠρώτησεν αὐτὸν ἀπὸ τῆς γῆς ἐπαναγαγεῖν ὀλίγον, καθίσας δὲ ἐκ τοῦ πλοίου ἐδίδασκεν τοὺς ὄχλους. ⁴ ὡς δὲ ἐπαύσατο λαλῶν, εἶπεν πρὸς τὸν Σίμωνα, Ἐπανάγαγε εἰς τὸ βάθος καὶ χαλάσατε τὰ δίκτυα ὑμῶν εἰς ἄγραν. ⁵ καὶ ἀποκριθεὶς Σίμων εἶπεν, Ἐπιστάτα, δι' ὅλης νυκτὸς κοπιάσαντες οὐδὲν ἐλάβομεν, ἐπὶ δὲ τῷ ῥήματί σου χαλάσω τὰ δίκτυα. ⁶ καὶ τοῦτο ποιήσαντες συνέκλεισαν πλῆθος ἰχθύων πολύ, διερρήσσετο δὲ τὰ δίκτυα αὐτῶν. ⁷ καὶ κατένευσαν τοῖς μετόχοις ἐν τῷ ἑτέρῳ πλοίῳ τοῦ ἐλθόντας συλλαβέσθαι αὐτοῖς· καὶ ἦλθαν, καὶ ἔπλησαν ἀμφότερα τὰ πλοῖα ὥστε βυθίζεσθαι αὐτά. ⁸ ἰδὼν δὲ Σίμων Πέτρος προσέπεσεν τοῖς γόνασιν Ἰησοῦ λέγων, Ἔξελθε ἀπ' ἐμοῦ, ὅτι ἀνὴρ ἁμαρτωλός εἰμι, κύριε· ⁹ θάμβος γὰρ περιέσχεν αὐτὸν καὶ πάντας τοὺς σὺν αὐτῷ ἐπὶ τῇ ἄγρᾳ τῶν ἰχθύων ὧν συνέλαβον, ¹⁰ ὁμοίως δὲ καὶ Ἰάκωβον καὶ Ἰωάννην υἱοὺς Ζεβεδαίου, οἳ ἦσαν κοινωνοὶ τῷ Σίμωνι. καὶ εἶπεν πρὸς τὸν Σίμωνα ὁ Ἰησοῦς, Μὴ φοβοῦ· ἀπὸ τοῦ νῦν ἀνθρώπους ἔσῃ ζωγρῶν. ¹¹ καὶ καταγαγόντες τὰ πλοῖα ἐπὶ τὴν γῆν ἀφέντες πάντα ἠκολούθησαν αὐτῷ.

English

¹ Once while Jesus was standing beside the lake of Gennesaret, and the crowd was pressing in on him to hear the word of God, ² he saw two boats there at the shore of the lake; the fishermen had gone out of them and were washing their nets. ³ He got into one of the boats, the one belonging to Simon, and asked him to put out a little way from the shore. Then he sat down and taught the crowds from the boat. ⁴ When he had finished speaking, he said to Simon, "Put out into the deep water and let down your nets for a catch." ⁵ Simon answered, "Master, we have worked all night long but have caught nothing. Yet if you say so, I will let down the nets." ⁶ When they had done this, they caught so many fish that their nets were beginning to break. ⁷ So they signaled their partners in the other boat to come and help them. And they came and filled both boats, so that they began to sink. ⁸ But when Simon Peter saw it, he fell down at Jesus' knees, saying, "Go away from me, Lord, for I am a sinful man!" ⁹ For he and all who were with him were amazed at the catch of fish that they had taken; ¹⁰ and so also were James and John, sons of Zebedee, who were partners with Simon. Then Jesus said to Simon, "Do not be afraid; from now on you will be catching people." ¹¹ When they had brought their boats to shore, they left everything and followed him.

JESUS RAISES WIDOW'S SON AT NAIN (7:11–17)

Greek

¹¹ Καὶ ἐγένετο ἐν τῷ ἑξῆς ἐπορεύθη εἰς πόλιν καλουμένην Ναΐν, καὶ συνεπορεύοντο αὐτῷ οἱ μαθηταὶ αὐτοῦ καὶ ὄχλος πολύς. ¹² ὡς δὲ ἤγγισεν τῇ πύλῃ τῆς πόλεως, καὶ ἰδοὺ ἐξεκομίζετο τεθνηκὼς μονογενὴς υἱὸς τῇ μητρὶ αὐτοῦ, καὶ αὐτὴ ἦν χήρα, καὶ ὄχλος τῆς πόλεως ἱκανὸς ἦν σὺν αὐτῇ. ¹³ καὶ ἰδὼν αὐτὴν ὁ κύριος ἐσπλαγχνίσθη ἐπ' αὐτῇ καὶ εἶπεν αὐτῇ, Μὴ κλαῖε. ¹⁴ καὶ προσελθὼν ἥψατο τῆς σοροῦ, οἱ δὲ βαστάζοντες ἔστησαν, καὶ εἶπεν, Νεανίσκε, σοὶ λέγω, ἐγέρθητι. ¹⁵ καὶ ἀνεκάθισεν ὁ νεκρὸς καὶ ἤρξατο λαλεῖν, καὶ ἔδωκεν αὐτὸν τῇ μητρὶ αὐτοῦ. ¹⁶ ἔλαβεν δὲ φόβος πάντας, καὶ ἐδόξαζον τὸν θεὸν λέγοντες ὅτι Προφήτης μέγας ἠγέρθη ἐν ἡμῖν, καὶ ὅτι Ἐπεσκέψατο ὁ θεὸς τὸν λαὸν αὐτοῦ. ¹⁷ καὶ ἐξῆλθεν ὁ λόγος οὗτος ἐν ὅλῃ τῇ Ἰουδαίᾳ περὶ αὐτοῦ καὶ πάσῃ τῇ περιχώρῳ.

English

¹¹ Soon afterwards he went to a town called Nain, and his disciples and a large crowd went with him. ¹² As he approached the gate of the town, a man who had died was being carried out. He was his mother's only son, and she was a widow; and with her was a large crowd from the town. ¹³ When the Lord saw her, he had compassion for her and said to her, "Do not weep." ¹⁴ Then he came forward and touched the bier, and the bearers stood still. And he said, "Young man, I say to you, rise!" ¹⁵ The dead man sat up and began to speak, and Jesus gave him to his mother. ¹⁶ Fear seized all of them; and they glorified God, saying, "A great prophet has risen among us!" and "God has looked favorably on his people!" ¹⁷ This word about him spread throughout Judea and all the surrounding country.

JESUS ANNOINTED BY A SINFUL WOMAN (7:36–50)

Greek

³⁶ Ἠρώτα δέ τις αὐτὸν τῶν Φαρισαίων ἵνα φάγῃ μετ' αὐτοῦ· καὶ εἰσελθὼν εἰς τὸν οἶκον τοῦ Φαρισαίου κατεκλίθη. ³⁷ καὶ ἰδοὺ γυνὴ ἥτις ἦν ἐν τῇ πόλει ἁμαρτωλός, καὶ ἐπιγνοῦσα ὅτι κατάκειται ἐν τῇ οἰκίᾳ τοῦ Φαρισαίου, κομίσασα ἀλάβαστρον μύρου ³⁸ καὶ στᾶσα ὀπίσω παρὰ τοὺς πόδας αὐτοῦ κλαίουσα, τοῖς δάκρυσιν ἤρξατο βρέχειν τοὺς πόδας αὐτοῦ καὶ ταῖς θριξὶν τῆς κεφαλῆς αὐτῆς ἐξέμασσεν, καὶ κατεφίλει τοὺς πόδας αὐτοῦ καὶ ἤλειφεν τῷ

μύρῳ. ³⁹ ἰδὼν δὲ ὁ Φαρισαῖος ὁ καλέσας αὐτὸν εἶπεν ἐν ἑαυτῷ λέγων, Οὗτος εἰ ἦν προφήτης, ἐγίνωσκεν ἂν τίς καὶ ποταπὴ ἡ γυνὴ ἥτις ἅπτεται αὐτοῦ, ὅτι ἁμαρτωλός ἐστιν. ⁴⁰ καὶ ἀποκριθεὶς ὁ Ἰησοῦς εἶπεν πρὸς αὐτόν, Σίμων, ἔχω σοί τι εἰπεῖν. ὁ δέ, Διδάσκαλε, εἰπέ, φησίν. ⁴¹ δύο χρεοφειλέται ἦσαν δανειστῇ τινι· ὁ εἷς ὤφειλεν δηνάρια πεντακόσια, ὁ δὲ ἕτερος πεντήκοντα. ⁴² μὴ ἐχόντων αὐτῶν ἀποδοῦναι ἀμφοτέροις ἐχαρίσατο. τίς οὖν αὐτῶν πλεῖον ἀγαπήσει αὐτόν; ⁴³ ἀποκριθεὶς Σίμων εἶπεν, Ὑπολαμβάνω ὅτι ᾧ τὸ πλεῖον ἐχαρίσατο. ὁ δὲ εἶπεν αὐτῷ, Ὀρθῶς ἔκρινας. ⁴⁴ καὶ στραφεὶς πρὸς τὴν γυναῖκα τῷ Σίμωνι ἔφη, Βλέπεις ταύτην τὴν γυναῖκα; εἰσῆλθόν σου εἰς τὴν οἰκίαν, ὕδωρ μοι ἐπὶ πόδας οὐκ ἔδωκας· αὕτη δὲ τοῖς δάκρυσιν ἔβρεξέν μου τοὺς πόδας καὶ ταῖς θριξὶν αὐτῆς ἐξέμαξεν. ⁴⁵ φίλημά μοι οὐκ ἔδωκας· αὕτη δὲ ἀφ᾽ ἧς εἰσῆλθον οὐ διέλιπεν καταφιλοῦσά μου τοὺς πόδας. ⁴⁶ ἐλαίῳ τὴν κεφαλήν μου οὐκ ἤλειψας· αὕτη δὲ μύρῳ ἤλειψεν τοὺς πόδας μου. ⁴⁷ οὗ χάριν, λέγω σοι, ἀφέωνται αἱ ἁμαρτίαι αὐτῆς αἱ πολλαί, ὅτι ἠγάπησεν πολύ· ᾧ δὲ ὀλίγον ἀφίεται, ὀλίγον ἀγαπᾷ. ⁴⁸ εἶπεν δὲ αὐτῇ, Ἀφέωνταί σου αἱ ἁμαρτίαι. ⁴⁹ καὶ ἤρξαντο οἱ συνανακείμενοι λέγειν ἐν ἑαυτοῖς, Τίς οὗτός ἐστιν ὃς καὶ ἁμαρτίας ἀφίησιν; ⁵⁰ εἶπεν δὲ πρὸς τὴν γυναῖκα, Ἡ πίστις σου σέσωκέν σε· πορεύου εἰς εἰρήνην.

English

³⁶ One of the Pharisees asked Jesus to eat with him, and he went into the Pharisee's house and took his place at the table. ³⁷ And a woman in the city, who was a sinner, having learned that he was eating in the Pharisee's house, brought an alabaster jar of ointment. ³⁸ She stood behind him at his feet, weeping, and began to bathe his feet with her tears and to dry them with her hair. Then she continued kissing his feet and anointing them with the ointment. ³⁹ Now when the Pharisee who had invited him saw it, he said to himself, "If this man were a prophet, he would have known who and what kind of woman this is who is touching him— that she is a sinner." ⁴⁰ Jesus spoke up and said to him, "Simon, I have something to say to you." "Teacher," he replied, "Speak." ⁴¹ "A certain creditor had two debtors; one owed five hundred denarii, and the other fifty. ⁴² When they could not pay, he canceled the debts for both of them. Now which of them will love him more?" ⁴³ Simon answered, "I suppose the one for whom he canceled the greater debt." And Jesus said to him, "You have judged rightly." ⁴⁴ Then turning toward the woman, he said to Simon, "Do you see this woman? I entered your house; you gave me no water for my feet, but she has bathed my feet with her tears and dried

them with her hair. [45] You gave me no kiss, but from the time I came in she has not stopped kissing my feet. [46] You did not anoint my head with oil, but she has anointed my feet with ointment. [47] Therefore, I tell you, her sins, which were many, have been forgiven; hence she has shown great love. But the one to whom little is forgiven, loves little." [48] Then he said to her, "Your sins are forgiven." [49] But those who were at the table with him began to say among themselves, "Who is this who even forgives sins?" [50] And he said to the woman, "Your faith has saved you; go in peace."

WOMEN ACCOMPANY JESUS (8:1–3)

Greek

[1] Καὶ ἐγένετο ἐν τῷ καθεξῆς καὶ αὐτὸς διώδευεν κατὰ πόλιν καὶ κώμην κηρύσσων καὶ εὐαγγελιζόμενος τὴν βασιλείαν τοῦ θεοῦ, καὶ οἱ δώδεκα σὺν αὐτῷ, [2] καὶ γυναῖκές τινες αἳ ἦσαν τεθεραπευμέναι ἀπὸ πνευμάτων πονηρῶν καὶ ἀσθενειῶν, Μαρία ἡ καλουμένη Μαγδαληνή, ἀφ' ἧς δαιμόνια ἑπτὰ ἐξεληλύθει, [3] καὶ Ἰωάννα γυνὴ Χουζᾶ ἐπιτρόπου Ἡρῴδου καὶ Σουσάννα καὶ ἕτεραι πολλαί, αἵτινες διηκόνουν αὐτοῖς ἐκ τῶν ὑπαρχόντων αὐταῖς.

English

[1] Soon afterwards he went on through cities and villages, proclaiming and bringing the good news of the kingdom of God. The twelve were with him, [2] as well as some women who had been cured of evil spirits and infirmities: Mary, called Magdalene, from whom seven demons had gone out, [3] and Joanna, the wife of Herod's steward Chuza, and Susanna, and many others, who provided for them out of their resources.

SAMARITAN VILLAGE REJECTS JESUS (9:51–56)

Greek

[51] Ἐγένετο δὲ ἐν τῷ συμπληροῦσθαι τὰς ἡμέρας τῆς ἀναλήμψεως αὐτοῦ καὶ αὐτὸς τὸ πρόσωπον ἐστήρισεν τοῦ πορεύεσθαι εἰς Ἰερουσαλήμ, [52] καὶ ἀπέστειλεν ἀγγέλους πρὸ προσώπου αὐτοῦ. καὶ πορευθέντες εἰσῆλθον εἰς κώμην Σαμαριτῶν, ὡς ἑτοιμάσαι αὐτῷ· [53] καὶ οὐκ ἐδέξαντο αὐτόν, ὅτι τὸ πρόσωπον αὐτοῦ ἦν πορευόμενον εἰς Ἰερουσαλήμ. [54] ἰδόντες δὲ οἱ μαθηταὶ

Ἰάκωβος καὶ Ἰωάννης εἶπαν, Κύριε, θέλεις εἴπωμεν πῦρ καταβῆναι ἀπὸ τοῦ οὐρανοῦ καὶ ἀναλῶσαι αὐτούς; ⁵⁵ στραφεὶς δὲ ἐπετίμησεν αὐτοῖς. ⁵⁶ καὶ ἐπορεύθησαν εἰς ἑτέραν κώμην.

English

⁵¹ When the days drew near for him to be taken up, he set his face to go to Jerusalem. ⁵² And he sent messengers ahead of him. On their way they entered a village of the Samaritans to make ready for him; ⁵³ but they did not receive him, because his face was set toward Jerusalem. ⁵⁴ When his disciples James and John saw it, they said, "Lord, do you want us to command fire to come down from heaven and consume them?" ⁵⁵ But he turned and rebuked them. ⁵⁶ Then they went on to another village.

RETURN OF THE SEVENTY (10:17–20)

Greek

17 Ὑπέστρεψαν δὲ οἱ ἑβδομήκοντα [δύο] μετὰ χαρᾶς λέγοντες, Κύριε, καὶ τὰ δαιμόνια ὑποτάσσεται ἡμῖν ἐν τῷ ὀνόματί σου. 18 εἶπεν δὲ αὐτοῖς, Ἐθεώρουν τὸν Σατανᾶν ὡς ἀστραπὴν ἐκ τοῦ οὐρανοῦ πεσόντα. 19 ἰδοὺ δέδωκα ὑμῖν τὴν ἐξουσίαν τοῦ πατεῖν ἐπάνω ὄφεων καὶ σκορπίων, καὶ ἐπὶ πᾶσαν τὴν δύναμιν τοῦ ἐχθροῦ, καὶ οὐδὲν ὑμᾶς οὐ μὴ ἀδικήσῃ. 20 πλὴν ἐν τούτῳ μὴ χαίρετε ὅτι τὰ πνεύματα ὑμῖν ὑποτάσσεται, χαίρετε δὲ ὅτι τὰ ὀνόματα ὑμῶν ἐγγέγραπται ἐν τοῖς οὐρανοῖς.

English

¹⁷ The seventy returned with joy, saying, "Lord, in your name even the demons submit to us!" ¹⁸ He said to them, "I watched Satan fall from heaven like a flash of lightning. ¹⁹ See, I have given you authority to tread on snakes and scorpions, and over all the power of the enemy; and nothing will hurt you. ²⁰ Nevertheless, do not rejoice at this, that the spirits submit to you, but rejoice that your names are written in heaven."

PARABLE OF THE GOOD SAMARITAN (10:29–37)

Greek

²⁹ ὁ δὲ θέλων δικαιῶσαι ἑαυτὸν εἶπεν πρὸς τὸν Ἰησοῦν, Καὶ τίς ἐστίν μου πλησίον; ³⁰ ὑπολαβὼν ὁ Ἰησοῦς εἶπεν, Ἄνθρωπός τις κατέβαινεν ἀπὸ Ἰερουσαλὴμ εἰς Ἰεριχὼ καὶ λῃσταῖς περιέπεσεν, οἳ καὶ ἐκδύσαντες αὐτὸν καὶ πληγὰς ἐπιθέντες ἀπῆλθον ἀφέντες ἡμιθανῆ. ³¹ κατὰ συγκυρίαν δὲ ἱερεύς τις κατέβαινεν ἐν τῇ ὁδῷ ἐκείνῃ, καὶ ἰδὼν αὐτὸν ἀντιπαρῆλθεν· ³² ὁμοίως δὲ καὶ Λευίτης [γενόμενος] κατὰ τὸν τόπον ἐλθὼν καὶ ἰδὼν ἀντιπαρῆλθεν. ³³ Σαμαρίτης δέ τις ὁδεύων ἦλθεν κατ' αὐτὸν καὶ ἰδὼν ἐσπλαγχνίσθη, ³⁴ καὶ προσελθὼν κατέδησεν τὰ τραύματα αὐτοῦ ἐπιχέων ἔλαιον καὶ οἶνον, ἐπιβιβάσας δὲ αὐτὸν ἐπὶ τὸ ἴδιον κτῆνος ἤγαγεν αὐτὸν εἰς πανδοχεῖον καὶ ἐπεμελήθη αὐτοῦ. ³⁵ καὶ ἐπὶ τὴν αὔριον ἐκβαλὼν ἔδωκεν δύο δηνάρια τῷ πανδοχεῖ καὶ εἶπεν, Ἐπιμελήθητι αὐτοῦ, καὶ ὅ τι ἂν προσδαπανήσῃς ἐγὼ ἐν τῷ ἐπανέρχεσθαί με ἀποδώσω σοι. ³⁶ τίς τούτων τῶν τριῶν πλησίον δοκεῖ σοι γεγονέναι τοῦ ἐμπεσόντος εἰς τοὺς λῃστάς; ³⁷ ὁ δὲ εἶπεν, Ὁ ποιήσας τὸ ἔλεος μετ' αὐτοῦ. εἶπεν δὲ αὐτῷ ὁ Ἰησοῦς, Πορεύου καὶ σὺ ποίει ὁμοίως.

English

²⁹ But wanting to justify himself, he asked Jesus, "And who is my neighbor?" ³⁰ Jesus replied, "A man was going down from Jerusalem to Jericho, and fell into the hands of robbers, who stripped him, beat him, and went away, leaving him half dead. ³¹ Now by chance a priest was going down that road; and when he saw him, he passed by on the other side. ³² So likewise a Levite, when he came to the place and saw him, passed by on the other side. ³³ But a Samaritan while traveling came near him; and when he saw him, he was moved with pity. ³⁴ He went to him and bandaged his wounds, having poured oil and wine on them. Then he put him on his own animal, brought him to an inn, and took care of him. ³⁵ The next day he took out two denarii, gave them to the innkeeper, and said, 'Take care of him; and when I come back, I will repay you whatever more you spend.' ³⁶ Which of these three, do you think, was a neighbor to the man who fell into the hands of the robbers?" ³⁷ He said, "The one who showed him mercy." Jesus said to him, "Go and do likewise."

JESUS VISITS MARTHA AND MARY (10:38–42)

Greek

³⁸ Ἐν δὲ τῷ πορεύεσθαι αὐτοὺς αὐτὸς εἰσῆλθεν εἰς κώμην τινά· γυνὴ δέ τις ὀνόματι Μάρθα ὑπεδέξατο αὐτόν. ³⁹ καὶ τῇδε ἦν ἀδελφὴ καλουμένη Μαριάμ, [ἣ] καὶ παρακαθεσθεῖσα πρὸς τοὺς πόδας τοῦ κυρίου ἤκουεν τὸν λόγον αὐτοῦ. ⁴⁰ ἡ δὲ Μάρθα περιεσπᾶτο περὶ πολλὴν διακονίαν· ἐπιστᾶσα δὲ εἶπεν, Κύριε, οὐ μέλει σοι ὅτι ἡ ἀδελφή μου μόνην με κατέλιπεν διακονεῖν; εἰπὲ οὖν αὐτῇ ἵνα μοι συναντιλάβηται. ⁴¹ ἀποκριθεὶς δὲ εἶπεν αὐτῇ ὁ κύριος, Μάρθα Μάρθα, μεριμνᾷς καὶ θορυβάζῃ περὶ πολλά, ⁴² ἑνὸς δέ ἐστιν χρεία Μαριὰμ γὰρ τὴν ἀγαθὴν μερίδα ἐξελέξατο ἥτις οὐκ ἀφαιρεθήσεται αὐτῆς.

English

³⁸ Now as they went on their way, he entered a certain village, where a woman named Martha welcomed him into her home. ³⁹ She had a sister named Mary, who sat at the Lord's feet and listened to what he was saying. ⁴⁰ But Martha was distracted by her many tasks; so she came to him and asked, "Lord, do you not care that my sister has left me to do all the work by myself? Tell her then to help me." ⁴¹ But the Lord answered her, "Martha, Martha, you are worried and distracted by many things; ⁴² there is need of only one thing. Mary has chosen the better part, which will not be taken away from her."

PARABLE OF FRIEND AT MIDNIGHT (11:5–8)

Greek

⁵ Καὶ εἶπεν πρὸς αὐτούς, Τίς ἐξ ὑμῶν ἕξει φίλον καὶ πορεύσεται πρὸς αὐτὸν μεσονυκτίου καὶ εἴπῃ αὐτῷ, Φίλε, χρῆσόν μοι τρεῖς ἄρτους, ⁶ ἐπειδὴ φίλος μου παρεγένετο ἐξ ὁδοῦ πρός με καὶ οὐκ ἔχω ὃ παραθήσω αὐτῷ· ⁷ κἀκεῖνος ἔσωθεν ἀποκριθεὶς εἴπῃ, Μή μοι κόπους πάρεχε· ἤδη ἡ θύρα κέκλεισται, καὶ τὰ παιδία μου μετ᾽ ἐμοῦ εἰς τὴν κοίτην εἰσίν· οὐ δύναμαι ἀναστὰς δοῦναί σοι. ⁸ λέγω ὑμῖν, εἰ καὶ οὐ δώσει αὐτῷ ἀναστὰς διὰ τὸ εἶναι φίλον αὐτοῦ, διά γε τὴν ἀναίδειαν αὐτοῦ ἐγερθεὶς δώσει αὐτῷ ὅσων χρῄζει.

English

⁵ And he said to them, "Suppose one of you has a friend, and you go to him at midnight and say to him, 'Friend, lend me three loaves of bread; ⁶ for a friend of mine has arrived, and I have nothing to set before him.' ⁷ And he answers from within, 'Do not bother me; the door has already been locked, and my children are with me in bed; I cannot get up and give you anything.' ⁸ I tell you, even though he will not get up and give him anything because he is his friend, at least because of his persistence he will get up and give him whatever he needs."

PARABLE OF THE RICH FOOL (12:13-21)

Greek

¹³ Εἶπεν δέ τις ἐκ τοῦ ὄχλου αὐτῷ, Διδάσκαλε, εἰπὲ τῷ ἀδελφῷ μου μερίσασθαι μετ᾽ ἐμοῦ τὴν κληρονομίαν. ¹⁴ ὁ δὲ εἶπεν αὐτῷ, Ἄνθρωπε, τίς με κατέστησεν κριτὴν ἢ μεριστὴν ἐφ᾽ ὑμᾶς; ¹⁵ εἶπεν δὲ πρὸς αὐτούς, Ὁρᾶτε καὶ φυλάσσεσθε ἀπὸ πάσης πλεονεξίας, ὅτι οὐκ ἐν τῷ περισσεύειν τινὶ ἡ ζωὴ αὐτοῦ ἐστιν ἐκ τῶν ὑπαρχόντων αὐτῷ. ¹⁶ Εἶπεν δὲ παραβολὴν πρὸς αὐτοὺς λέγων, Ἀνθρώπου τινὸς πλουσίου εὐφόρησεν ἡ χώρα. ¹⁷ καὶ διελογίζετο ἐν ἑαυτῷ λέγων, Τί ποιήσω, ὅτι οὐκ ἔχω ποῦ συνάξω τοὺς καρπούς μου; ¹⁸ καὶ εἶπεν, Τοῦτο ποιήσω· καθελῶ μου τὰς ἀποθήκας καὶ μείζονας οἰκοδομήσω, καὶ συνάξω ἐκεῖ πάντα τὸν σῖτον καὶ τὰ ἀγαθά μου, ¹⁹ καὶ ἐρῶ τῇ ψυχῇ μου, Ψυχή, ἔχεις πολλὰ ἀγαθὰ κείμενα εἰς ἔτη πολλά· ἀναπαύου, φάγε, πίε, εὐφραίνου. ²⁰ εἶπεν δὲ αὐτῷ ὁ θεός, Ἄφρων, ταύτῃ τῇ νυκτὶ τὴν ψυχήν σου ἀπαιτοῦσιν ἀπὸ σοῦ· ἃ δὲ ἡτοίμασας, τίνι ἔσται; ²¹ οὕτως ὁ θησαυρίζων ἑαυτῷ καὶ μὴ εἰς θεὸν πλουτῶν.

English

¹³ Someone in the crowd said to him, "Teacher, tell my brother to divide the family inheritance with me." ¹⁴ But he said to him, "Friend, who set me to be a judge or arbitrator over you?" ¹⁵ And he said to them, "Take care! Be on your guard against all kinds of greed; for one's life does not consist in the abundance of possessions." ¹⁶ Then he told them a parable: "The land of a rich man produced abundantly. ¹⁷ And he thought to himself, 'What should I do, for I have no place to store my crops?' ¹⁸ Then he said, 'I will do this: I will pull down my barns and build larger ones, and there I will store all my grain and my goods. ¹⁹ And I will say to

my soul, 'Soul, you have ample goods laid up for many years; relax, eat, drink, be merry.' [20] But God said to him, 'You fool! This very night your life is being demanded of you. And the things you have prepared, whose will they be?' [21] So it is with those who store up treasures for themselves but are not rich toward God.'"

REPENT OR PERISH (13:1–5)

Greek

[1] Παρῆσαν δέ τινες ἐν αὐτῷ τῷ καιρῷ ἀπαγγέλλοντες αὐτῷ περὶ τῶν Γαλιλαίων ὧν τὸ αἷμα Πιλᾶτος ἔμιξεν μετὰ τῶν θυσιῶν αὐτῶν. [2] καὶ ἀποκριθεὶς εἶπεν αὐτοῖς, Δοκεῖτε ὅτι οἱ Γαλιλαῖοι οὗτοι ἁμαρτωλοὶ παρὰ πάντας τοὺς Γαλιλαίους ἐγένοντο, ὅτι ταῦτα πεπόνθασιν; [3] οὐχί, λέγω ὑμῖν, ἀλλ᾽ ἐὰν μὴ μετανοῆτε πάντες ὁμοίως ἀπολεῖσθε. [4] ἢ ἐκεῖνοι οἱ δέκα ὀκτὼ ἐφ᾽ οὓς ἔπεσεν ὁ πύργος ἐν τῷ Σιλωὰμ καὶ ἀπέκτεινεν αὐτούς, δοκεῖτε ὅτι αὐτοὶ ὀφειλέται ἐγένοντο παρὰ πάντας τοὺς ἀνθρώπους τοὺς κατοικοῦντας Ἰερουσαλήμ; [5] οὐχί, λέγω ὑμῖν, ἀλλ᾽ ἐὰν μὴ μετανοῆτε πάντες ὡσαύτως ἀπολεῖσθε.

English

[1] At that very time there were some present who told him about the Galileans whose blood Pilate had mingled with their sacrifices. [2] He asked them, "Do you think that because these Galileans suffered in this way they were worse sinners than all other Galileans? [3] No, I tell you; but unless you repent, you will all perish as they did. [4] Or those eighteen who were killed when the tower of Siloam fell on them—do you think that they were worse offenders than all the others living in Jerusalem? [5] No, I tell you; but unless you repent, you will all perish just as they did."

PARABLE OF THE BARREN FIG TREE (13:6–9)

Greek

[6] Ἔλεγεν δὲ ταύτην τὴν παραβολήν· Συκῆν εἶχέν τις πεφυτευμένην ἐν τῷ ἀμπελῶνι αὐτοῦ, καὶ ἦλθεν ζητῶν καρπὸν ἐν αὐτῇ καὶ οὐχ εὗρεν. [7] εἶπεν δὲ πρὸς τὸν ἀμπελουργόν, Ἰδοὺ τρία ἔτη ἀφ᾽ οὗ ἔρχομαι ζητῶν καρπὸν ἐν τῇ συκῇ ταύτῃ καὶ οὐχ εὑρίσκω. ἔκκοψον [οὖν] αὐτήν· ἱνατί καὶ τὴν

γῆν καταργεῖ; 8 ὁ δὲ ἀποκριθεὶς λέγει αὐτῷ, Κύριε, ἄφες αὐτὴν καὶ τοῦτο τὸ ἔτος, ἕως ὅτου σκάψω περὶ αὐτὴν καὶ βάλω κόπρια· 9 κἂν μὲν ποιήσῃ καρπὸν εἰς τὸ μέλλον, εἰ δὲ μή γε, ἐκκόψεις αὐτήν.

English

⁶ Then he told this parable: "A man had a fig tree planted in his vineyard; and he came looking for fruit on it and found none. ⁷ So he said to the gardener, 'See here! For three years I have come looking for fruit on this fig tree, and still I find none. Cut it down! Why should it be wasting the soil?' ⁸ He replied, 'Sir, let it alone for one more year, until I dig around it and put manure on it. ⁹ If it bears fruit next year, well and good; but if not, you can cut it down.'"

JESUS HEALS A CRIPPLED WOMAN (13:10-17)

Greek

¹⁰ Ἦν δὲ διδάσκων ἐν μιᾷ τῶν συναγωγῶν ἐν τοῖς σάββασιν. ¹¹ καὶ ἰδοὺ γυνὴ πνεῦμα ἔχουσα ἀσθενείας ἔτη δέκα ὀκτώ, καὶ ἦν συγκύπτουσα καὶ μὴ δυναμένη ἀνακύψαι εἰς τὸ παντελές. ¹² ἰδὼν δὲ αὐτὴν ὁ Ἰησοῦς προσεφώνησεν καὶ εἶπεν αὐτῇ, Γύναι, ἀπολέλυσαι τῆς ἀσθενείας σου, ¹³ καὶ ἐπέθηκεν αὐτῇ τὰς χεῖρας· καὶ παραχρῆμα ἀνωρθώθη, καὶ ἐδόξαζεν τὸν θεόν. ¹⁴ ἀποκριθεὶς δὲ ὁ ἀρχισυνάγωγος, ἀγανακτῶν ὅτι τῷ σαββάτῳ ἐθεράπευσεν ὁ Ἰησοῦς, ἔλεγεν τῷ ὄχλῳ ὅτι Ἓξ ἡμέραι εἰσὶν ἐν αἷς δεῖ ἐργάζεσθαι· ἐν αὐταῖς οὖν ἐρχόμενοι θεραπεύεσθε καὶ μὴ τῇ ἡμέρᾳ τοῦ σαββάτου. ¹⁵ ἀπεκρίθη δὲ αὐτῷ ὁ κύριος καὶ εἶπεν, Ὑποκριταί, ἕκαστος ὑμῶν τῷ σαββάτῳ οὐ λύει τὸν βοῦν αὐτοῦ ἢ τὸν ὄνον ἀπὸ τῆς φάτνης καὶ ἀπαγαγὼν ποτίζει; ¹⁶ ταύτην δὲ θυγατέρα Ἀβραὰμ οὖσαν, ἣν ἔδησεν ὁ Σατανᾶς ἰδοὺ δέκα καὶ ὀκτὼ ἔτη, οὐκ ἔδει λυθῆναι ἀπὸ τοῦ δεσμοῦ τούτου τῇ ἡμέρᾳ τοῦ σαββάτου; ¹⁷ καὶ ταῦτα λέγοντος αὐτοῦ κατῃσχύνοντο πάντες οἱ ἀντικείμενοι αὐτῷ, καὶ πᾶς ὁ ὄχλος ἔχαιρεν ἐπὶ πᾶσιν τοῖς ἐνδόξοις τοῖς γινομένοις ὑπ' αὐτοῦ.

English

¹⁰ Now he was teaching in one of the synagogues on the sabbath. ¹¹ And just then there appeared a woman with a spirit that had crippled her for eighteen years. She was bent over and was quite unable to stand up straight. ¹² When Jesus saw her, he called her over and said, "Woman,

you are set free from your ailment." [13] When he laid his hands on her, immediately she stood up straight and began praising God. [14] But the leader of the synagogue, indignant because Jesus had cured on the sabbath, kept saying to the crowd, "There are six days on which work ought to be done; come on those days and be cured, and not on the sabbath day." [15] But the Lord answered him and said, "You hypocrites! Does not each of you on the sabbath untie his ox or his donkey from the manger, and lead it away to give it water? [16] And ought not this woman, a daughter of Abraham whom Satan bound for eighteen long years, be set free from this bondage on the sabbath day?" [17] When he said this, all his opponents were put to shame; and the entire crowd was rejoicing at all the wonderful things that he was doing.

JESUS HEALS MAN WITH DROPSY (14:1–6)

Greek

[1] Καὶ ἐγένετο ἐν τῷ ἐλθεῖν αὐτὸν εἰς οἶκόν τινος τῶν ἀρχόντων [τῶν] Φαρισαίων σαββάτῳ φαγεῖν ἄρτον καὶ αὐτοὶ ἦσαν παρατηρούμενοι αὐτόν. [2] καὶ ἰδοὺ ἄνθρωπός τις ἦν ὑδρωπικὸς ἔμπροσθεν αὐτοῦ. [3] καὶ ἀποκριθεὶς ὁ Ἰησοῦς εἶπεν πρὸς τοὺς νομικοὺς καὶ Φαρισαίους λέγων, Ἔξεστιν τῷ σαββάτῳ θεραπεῦσαι ἢ οὔ; [4] οἱ δὲ ἡσύχασαν. καὶ ἐπιλαβόμενος ἰάσατο αὐτὸν καὶ ἀπέλυσεν. [5] καὶ πρὸς αὐτοὺς εἶπεν, Τίνος ὑμῶν υἱὸς ἢ βοῦς εἰς φρέαρ πεσεῖται, καὶ οὐκ εὐθέως ἀνασπάσει αὐτὸν ἐν ἡμέρᾳ τοῦ σαββάτου; [6] καὶ οὐκ ἴσχυσαν ἀνταποκριθῆναι πρὸς ταῦτα.

English

[1] On one occasion when Jesus was going to the house of a leader of the Pharisees to eat a meal on the sabbath, they were watching him closely. [2] Just then, in front of him, there was a man who had dropsy. [3] And Jesus asked the lawyers and Pharisees, "Is it lawful to cure people on the sabbath, or not?" [4] But they were silent. So Jesus took him and healed him, and sent him away. [5] Then he said to them, "If one of you has a child or an ox that has fallen into a well, will you not immediately pull it out on a sabbath day?" [6] And they could not reply to this.

HUMILITY AND HOSPITALITY (14:7–14)

Greek

7 Ἔλεγεν δὲ πρὸς τοὺς κεκλημένους παραβολήν, ἐπέχων πῶς τὰς πρωτοκλισίας ἐξελέγοντο, λέγων πρὸς αὐτούς, 8 Ὅταν κληθῇς ὑπό τινος εἰς γάμους, μὴ κατακλιθῇς εἰς τὴν πρωτοκλισίαν, μήποτε ἐντιμότερός σου ᾖ κεκλημένος ὑπ' αὐτοῦ, 9 καὶ ἐλθὼν ὁ σὲ καὶ αὐτὸν καλέσας ἐρεῖ σοι, Δὸς τούτῳ τόπον, καὶ τότε ἄρξῃ μετὰ αἰσχύνης τὸν ἔσχατον τόπον κατέχειν. 10 ἀλλ' ὅταν κληθῇς πορευθεὶς ἀνάπεσε εἰς τὸν ἔσχατον τόπον, ἵνα ὅταν ἔλθῃ ὁ κεκληκώς σε ἐρεῖ σοι, Φίλε, προσανάβηθι ἀνώτερον· τότε ἔσται σοι δόξα ἐνώπιον πάντων τῶν συνανακειμένων σοι. 11 ὅτι πᾶς ὁ ὑψῶν ἑαυτὸν ταπεινωθήσεται καὶ ὁ ταπεινῶν ἑαυτὸν ὑψωθήσεται. 12 Ἔλεγεν δὲ καὶ τῷ κεκληκότι αὐτόν, Ὅταν ποιῇς ἄριστον ἢ δεῖπνον, μὴ φώνει τοὺς φίλους σου μηδὲ τοὺς ἀδελφούς σου μηδὲ τοὺς συγγενεῖς σου μηδὲ γείτονας πλουσίους, μήποτε καὶ αὐτοὶ ἀντικαλέσωσίν σε καὶ γένηται ἀνταπόδομά σοι. 13 ἀλλ' ὅταν δοχὴν ποιῇς, κάλει πτωχούς, ἀναπείρους, χωλούς, τυφλούς· 14 καὶ μακάριος ἔσῃ, ὅτι οὐκ ἔχουσιν ἀνταποδοῦναί σοι, ἀνταποδοθήσεται γάρ σοι ἐν τῇ ἀναστάσει τῶν δικαίων.

English

7 When he noticed how the guests chose the places of honor, he told them a parable. 8 "When you are invited by someone to a wedding banquet, do not sit down at the place of honor, in case someone more distinguished than you has been invited by your host; 9 and the host who invited both of you may come and say to you, 'Give this person your place,' and then in disgrace you would start to take the lowest place. 10 But when you are invited, go and sit down at the lowest place, so that when your host comes, he may say to you, 'Friend, move up higher'; then you will be honored in the presence of all who sit at the table with you. 11 For all who exalt themselves will be humbled, and those who humble themselves will be exalted." 12 He said also to the one who had invited him, "When you give a luncheon or a dinner, do not invite your friends or your brothers or your relatives or rich neighbors, in case they may invite you in return, and you would be repaid. 13 But when you give a banquet, invite the poor, the crippled, the lame, and the blind. 14 And you will be blessed, because they cannot repay you, for you will be repaid at the resurrection of the righteous."

COST OF DISCIPLESHIP (14:28-33)

Greek

²⁸ τίς γὰρ ἐξ ὑμῶν θέλων πύργον οἰκοδομῆσαι οὐχὶ πρῶτον καθίσας ψηφίζει τὴν δαπάνην, εἰ ἔχει εἰς ἀπαρτισμόν; ²⁹ ἵνα μήποτε θέντος αὐτοῦ θεμέλιον καὶ μὴ ἰσχύοντος ἐκτελέσαι πάντες οἱ θεωροῦντες ἄρξωνται αὐτῷ ἐμπαίζειν ³⁰ λέγοντες ὅτι Οὗτος ὁ ἄνθρωπος ἤρξατο οἰκοδομεῖν καὶ οὐκ ἴσχυσεν ἐκτελέσαι. ³¹ ἢ τίς βασιλεὺς πορευόμενος ἑτέρῳ βασιλεῖ συμβαλεῖν εἰς πόλεμον οὐχὶ καθίσας πρῶτον βουλεύσεται εἰ δυνατός ἐστιν ἐν δέκα χιλιάσιν ὑπαντῆσαι τῷ μετὰ εἴκοσι χιλιάδων ἐρχομένῳ ἐπ᾽ αὐτόν; ³² εἰ δὲ μήγε, ἔτι αὐτοῦ πόρρω ὄντος πρεσβείαν ἀποστείλας ἐρωτᾷ τὰ πρὸς εἰρήνην. ³³ οὕτως οὖν πᾶς ἐξ ὑμῶν ὃς οὐκ ἀποτάσσεται πᾶσιν τοῖς ἑαυτοῦ ὑπάρχουσιν οὐ δύναται εἶναί μου μαθητής.

English

²⁸ For which of you, intending to build a tower, does not first sit down and estimate the cost, to see whether he has enough to complete it? ²⁹ Otherwise, when he has laid a foundation and is not able to finish, all who see it will begin to ridicule him, ³⁰ saying, 'This fellow began to build and was not able to finish.' ³¹ Or what king, going out to wage war against another king, will not sit down first and consider whether he is able with ten thousand to oppose the one who comes against him with twenty thousand? ³² If he cannot, then, while the other is still far away, he sends a delegation and asks for the terms of peace. ³³ So therefore, none of you can become my disciple if you do not give up all your possessions.

PARABLE OF LOST COIN (15:8-10)

Greek

⁸ Ἢ τίς γυνὴ δραχμὰς ἔχουσα δέκα, ἐὰν ἀπολέσῃ δραχμὴν μίαν, οὐχὶ ἅπτει λύχνον καὶ σαροῖ τὴν οἰκίαν καὶ ζητεῖ ἐπιμελῶς ἕως οὗ εὕρῃ; ⁹ καὶ εὑροῦσα συγκαλεῖ τὰς φίλας καὶ γείτονας λέγουσα, Συγχάρητέ μοι, ὅτι εὗρον τὴν δραχμὴν ἣν ἀπώλεσα. ¹⁰ οὕτως, λέγω ὑμῖν, γίνεται χαρὰ ἐνώπιον τῶν ἀγγέλων τοῦ θεοῦ ἐπὶ ἑνὶ ἁμαρτωλῷ μετανοοῦντι.

English

⁸ "Or what woman having ten silver coins, if she loses one of them, does not light a lamp, sweep the house, and search carefully until she finds it? ⁹ When she has found it, she calls together her friends and neighbors, saying, 'Rejoice with me, for I have found the coin that I had lost.' ¹⁰ Just so, I tell you, there is joy in the presence of the angels of God over one sinner who repents."

PARABLE OF PRODIGAL SON (15:11–32)

Greek

¹¹ Εἶπεν δέ, Ἄνθρωπός τις εἶχεν δύο υἱούς. ¹² καὶ εἶπεν ὁ νεώτερος αὐτῶν τῷ πατρί, Πάτερ, δός μοι τὸ ἐπιβάλλον μέρος τῆς οὐσίας. ὁ δὲ διεῖλεν αὐτοῖς τὸν βίον. ¹³ καὶ μετ' οὐ πολλὰς ἡμέρας συναγαγὼν ἅπαντα ὁ νεώτερος υἱὸς ἀπεδήμησεν εἰς χώραν μακράν, καὶ ἐκεῖ διεσκόρπισεν τὴν οὐσίαν αὐτοῦ ζῶν ἀσώτως. ¹⁴ δαπανήσαντος δὲ αὐτοῦ πάντα ἐγένετο λιμὸς ἰσχυρὰ κατὰ τὴν χώραν ἐκείνην, καὶ αὐτὸς ἤρξατο ὑστερεῖσθαι. ¹⁵ καὶ πορευθεὶς ἐκολλήθη ἑνὶ τῶν πολιτῶν τῆς χώρας ἐκείνης, καὶ ἔπεμψεν αὐτὸν εἰς τοὺς ἀγροὺς αὐτοῦ βόσκειν χοίρους· ¹⁶ καὶ ἐπεθύμει χορτασθῆναι ἐκ τῶν κερατίων ὧν ἤσθιον οἱ χοῖροι, καὶ οὐδεὶς ἐδίδου αὐτῷ. ¹⁷ εἰς ἑαυτὸν δὲ ἐλθὼν ἔφη, Πόσοι μίσθιοι τοῦ πατρός μου περισσεύονται ἄρτων, ἐγὼ δὲ λιμῷ ὧδε ἀπόλλυμαι. ¹⁸ ἀναστὰς πορεύσομαι πρὸς τὸν πατέρα μου καὶ ἐρῶ αὐτῷ, Πάτερ, ἥμαρτον εἰς τὸν οὐρανὸν καὶ ἐνώπιόν σου, ¹⁹ οὐκέτι εἰμὶ ἄξιος κληθῆναι υἱός σου· ποίησόν με ὡς ἕνα τῶν μισθίων σου. ²⁰ καὶ ἀναστὰς ἦλθεν πρὸς τὸν πατέρα ἑαυτοῦ. ἔτι δὲ αὐτοῦ μακρὰν ἀπέχοντος εἶδεν αὐτὸν ὁ πατὴρ αὐτοῦ καὶ ἐσπλαγχνίσθη καὶ δραμὼν ἐπέπεσεν ἐπὶ τὸν τράχηλον αὐτοῦ καὶ κατεφίλησεν αὐτόν. ²¹ εἶπεν δὲ ὁ υἱὸς αὐτῷ, Πάτερ, ἥμαρτον εἰς τὸν οὐρανὸν καὶ ἐνώπιόν σου, οὐκέτι εἰμὶ ἄξιος κληθῆναι υἱός σου. ²² εἶπεν δὲ ὁ πατὴρ πρὸς τοὺς δούλους αὐτοῦ, Ταχὺ ἐξενέγκατε στολὴν τὴν πρώτην καὶ ἐνδύσατε αὐτόν, καὶ δότε δακτύλιον εἰς τὴν χεῖρα αὐτοῦ καὶ ὑποδήματα εἰς τοὺς πόδας, ²³ καὶ φέρετε τὸν μόσχον τὸν σιτευτόν, θύσατε καὶ φαγόντες εὐφρανθῶμεν, ²⁴ ὅτι οὗτος ὁ υἱός μου νεκρὸς ἦν καὶ ἀνέζησεν, ἦν ἀπολωλὼς καὶ εὑρέθη. καὶ ἤρξαντο εὐφραίνεσθαι. ²⁵ Ἦν δὲ ὁ υἱὸς αὐτοῦ ὁ πρεσβύτερος ἐν ἀγρῷ· καὶ ὡς ἐρχόμενος ἤγγισεν τῇ οἰκίᾳ, ἤκουσεν συμφωνίας καὶ χορῶν, ²⁶ καὶ προσκαλεσάμενος ἕνα τῶν παίδων ἐπυνθάνετο τί ἂν εἴη ταῦτα. ²⁷ ὁ δὲ εἶπεν αὐτῷ ὅτι Ὁ ἀδελφός σου ἥκει, καὶ ἔθυσεν ὁ πατήρ σου τὸν μόσχον τὸν σιτευτόν, ὅτι ὑγιαίνοντα αὐτὸν

ἀπέλαβεν. ²⁸ ὠργίσθη δὲ καὶ οὐκ ἤθελεν εἰσελθεῖν. ὁ δὲ πατὴρ αὐτοῦ
ἐξελθὼν παρεκάλει αὐτόν. ²⁹ ὁ δὲ ἀποκριθεὶς εἶπεν τῷ πατρὶ αὐτοῦ, Ἰδοὺ
τοσαῦτα ἔτη δουλεύω σοι καὶ οὐδέποτε ἐντολήν σου παρῆλθον, καὶ ἐμοὶ
οὐδέποτε ἔδωκας ἔριφον ἵνα μετὰ τῶν φίλων μου εὐφρανθῶ· ³⁰ ὅτε δὲ ὁ
υἱός σου οὗτος ὁ καταφαγών σου τὸν βίον μετὰ πορνῶν ἦλθεν, ἔθυσας αὐτῷ
τὸν σιτευτὸν μόσχον. ³¹ ὁ δὲ εἶπεν αὐτῷ, Τέκνον, σὺ πάντοτε μετ' ἐμοῦ
εἶ, καὶ πάντα τὰ ἐμὰ σά ἐστιν· ³² εὐφρανθῆναι δὲ καὶ χαρῆναι ἔδει, ὅτι ὁ
ἀδελφός σου οὗτος νεκρὸς ἦν καὶ ἔζησεν, καὶ ἀπολωλὼς καὶ εὑρέθη.

English

¹¹ Then Jesus said, "There was a man who had two sons. ¹² The younger
of them said to his father, 'Father, give me the share of the property that
will belong to me.' So he divided his property between them. ¹³ A few
days later the younger son gathered all he had and traveled to a dis-
tant country, and there he squandered his property in dissolute living.
¹⁴ When he had spent everything, a severe famine took place throughout
that country, and he began to be in need. ¹⁵ So he went and hired himself
out to one of the citizens of that country, who sent him to his fields to
feed the pigs. ¹⁶ He would gladly have filled himself with the pods that
the pigs were eating; and no one gave him anything. ¹⁷ But when he
came to himself he said, 'How many of my father's hired hands have
bread enough and to spare, but here I am dying of hunger! ¹⁸ I will get up
and go to my father, and I will say to him, "Father, I have sinned against
heaven and before you; ¹⁹ I am no longer worthy to be called your son;
treat me like one of your hired hands."' ²⁰ So he set off and went to his
father. But while he was still far off, his father saw him and was filled
with compassion; he ran and put his arms around him and kissed him.
²¹ Then the son said to him, 'Father, I have sinned against heaven and
before you; I am no longer worthy to be called your son.' ²² But the father
said to his slaves, 'Quickly, bring out a robe—the best one—and put it
on him; put a ring on his finger and sandals on his feet. ²³ And get the
fatted calf and kill it, and let us eat and celebrate; ²⁴ for this son of mine
was dead and is alive again; he was lost and is found!' And they began
to celebrate. ²⁵ "Now his elder son was in the field; and when he came
and approached the house, he heard music and dancing. ²⁶ He called one
of the slaves and asked what was going on. ²⁷ He replied, 'Your brother
has come, and your father has killed the fatted calf, because he has got
him back safe and sound.' ²⁸ Then he became angry and refused to go

in. His father came out and began to plead with him. ²⁹ But he answered his father, 'Listen! For all these years I have been working like a slave for you, and I have never disobeyed your command; yet you have never given me even a young goat so that I might celebrate with my friends. ³⁰ But when this son of yours came back, who has devoured your property with prostitutes, you killed the fatted calf for him!' ³¹ Then the father said to him, 'Son, you are always with me, and all that is mine is yours. ³² But we had to celebrate and rejoice, because this brother of yours was dead and has come to life; he was lost and has been found.'"

PARABLE OF DISHONEST MANAGER (16:1–12)

Greek

¹ Ἔλεγεν δὲ καὶ πρὸς τοὺς μαθητάς, Ἄνθρωπός τις ἦν πλούσιος ὃς εἶχεν οἰκονόμον, καὶ οὗτος διεβλήθη αὐτῷ ὡς διασκορπίζων τὰ ὑπάρχοντα αὐτοῦ. ² καὶ φωνήσας αὐτὸν εἶπεν αὐτῷ, Τί τοῦτο ἀκούω περὶ σοῦ; ἀπόδος τὸν λόγον τῆς οἰκονομίας σου, οὐ γὰρ δύνῃ ἔτι οἰκονομεῖν. ³ εἶπεν δὲ ἐν ἑαυτῷ ὁ οἰκονόμος, Τί ποιήσω, ὅτι ὁ κύριός μου ἀφαιρεῖται τὴν οἰκονομίαν ἀπ' ἐμοῦ; σκάπτειν οὐκ ἰσχύω, ἐπαιτεῖν αἰσχύνομαι. ⁴ ἔγνων τί ποιήσω, ἵνα ὅταν μετασταθῶ ἐκ τῆς οἰκονομίας δέξωνταί με εἰς τοὺς οἴκους ἑαυτῶν. ⁵ καὶ προσκαλεσάμενος ἕνα ἕκαστον τῶν χρεοφειλετῶν τοῦ κυρίου ἑαυτοῦ ἔλεγεν τῷ πρώτῳ, Πόσον ὀφείλεις τῷ κυρίῳ μου; ⁶ ὁ δὲ εἶπεν, Ἑκατὸν βάτους ἐλαίου. ὁ δὲ εἶπεν αὐτῷ, Δέξαι σου τὰ γράμματα καὶ καθίσας ταχέως γράψον πεντήκοντα. ⁷ ἔπειτα ἑτέρῳ εἶπεν, Σὺ δὲ πόσον ὀφείλεις; ὁ δὲ εἶπεν, Ἑκατὸν κόρους σίτου. λέγει αὐτῷ, Δέξαι σου τὰ γράμματα καὶ γράψον ὀγδοήκοντα. ⁸ καὶ ἐπήνεσεν ὁ κύριος τὸν οἰκονόμον τῆς ἀδικίας ὅτι φρονίμως ἐποίησεν· ὅτι οἱ υἱοὶ τοῦ αἰῶνος τούτου φρονιμώτεροι ὑπὲρ τοὺς υἱοὺς τοῦ φωτὸς εἰς τὴν γενεὰν τὴν ἑαυτῶν εἰσιν. ⁹ Καὶ ἐγὼ ὑμῖν λέγω, ἑαυτοῖς ποιήσατε φίλους ἐκ τοῦ μαμωνᾶ τῆς ἀδικίας, ἵνα ὅταν ἐκλίπῃ δέξωνται ὑμᾶς εἰς τὰς αἰωνίους σκηνάς. ¹⁰ ὁ πιστὸς ἐν ἐλαχίστῳ καὶ ἐν πολλῷ πιστός ἐστιν, καὶ ὁ ἐν ἐλαχίστῳ ἄδικος καὶ ἐν πολλῷ ἄδικός ἐστιν. ¹¹ εἰ οὖν ἐν τῷ ἀδίκῳ μαμωνᾷ πιστοὶ οὐκ ἐγένεσθε, τὸ ἀληθινὸν τίς ὑμῖν πιστεύσει; ¹² καὶ εἰ ἐν τῷ ἀλλοτρίῳ πιστοὶ οὐκ ἐγένεσθε, τὸ ὑμέτερον τίς δώσει ὑμῖν;

English

¹ Then Jesus said to the disciples, "There was a rich man who had a manager, and charges were brought to him that this man was squandering his property. ² So he summoned him and said to him, 'What is this that I hear about you? Give me an accounting of your management, because you cannot be my manager any longer.' ³ Then the manager said to himself, 'What will I do, now that my master is taking the position away from me? I am not strong enough to dig, and I am ashamed to beg. ⁴ I have decided what to do so that, when I am dismissed as manager, people may welcome me into their homes.' ⁵ So, summoning his master's debtors one by one, he asked the first, 'How much do you owe my master?' ⁶ He answered, 'A hundred jugs of olive oil.' He said to him, 'Take your bill, sit down quickly, and make it fifty.' ⁷ Then he asked another, 'And how much do you owe?' He replied, 'A hundred containers of wheat.' He said to him, 'Take your bill and make it eighty.' ⁸ And his master commended the dishonest manager because he had acted shrewdly; for the children of this age are more shrewd in dealing with their own generation than are the children of light. ⁹ And I tell you, make friends for yourselves by means of dishonest wealth so that when it is gone, they may welcome you into the eternal homes. ¹⁰ Whoever is faithful in a very little is faithful also in much; and whoever is dishonest in a very little is dishonest also in much. ¹¹ If then you have not been faithful with the dishonest wealth, who will entrust to you the true riches? ¹² And if you have not been faithful with what belongs to another, who will give you what is your own?"

PARABLE OF RICH MAN AND LAZARUS (16:19–31)

Greek

¹⁹ Ἄνθρωπος δέ τις ἦν πλούσιος, καὶ ἐνεδιδύσκετο πορφύραν καὶ βύσσον εὐφραινόμενος καθ' ἡμέραν λαμπρῶς. ²⁰ πτωχὸς δέ τις ὀνόματι Λάζαρος ἐβέβλητο πρὸς τὸν πυλῶνα αὐτοῦ εἱλκωμένος ²¹ καὶ ἐπιθυμῶν χορτασθῆναι ἀπὸ τῶν πιπτόντων ἀπὸ τῆς τραπέζης τοῦ πλουσίου· ἀλλὰ καὶ οἱ κύνες ἐρχόμενοι ἐπέλειχον τὰ ἕλκη αὐτοῦ. ²² ἐγένετο δὲ ἀποθανεῖν τὸν πτωχὸν καὶ ἀπενεχθῆναι αὐτὸν ὑπὸ τῶν ἀγγέλων εἰς τὸν κόλπον Ἀβραάμ· ἀπέθανεν δὲ καὶ ὁ πλούσιος καὶ ἐτάφη. ²³ καὶ ἐν τῷ ᾅδῃ ἐπάρας τοὺς ὀφθαλμοὺς αὐτοῦ, ὑπάρχων ἐν βασάνοις, ὁρᾷ Ἀβραὰμ ἀπὸ μακρόθεν καὶ Λάζαρον ἐν

τοῖς κόλποις αὐτοῦ. ²⁴ καὶ αὐτὸς φωνήσας εἶπεν, Πάτερ Ἀβραάμ, ἐλέησόν
με καὶ πέμψον Λάζαρον ἵνα βάψῃ τὸ ἄκρον τοῦ δακτύλου αὐτοῦ ὕδατος
καὶ καταψύξῃ τὴν γλῶσσάν μου, ὅτι ὀδυνῶμαι ἐν τῇ φλογὶ ταύτῃ. ²⁵ εἶπεν
δὲ Ἀβραάμ, Τέκνον, μνήσθητι ὅτι ἀπέλαβες τὰ ἀγαθά σου ἐν τῇ ζωῇ σου,
καὶ Λάζαρος ὁμοίως τὰ κακά· νῦν δὲ ὧδε παρακαλεῖται σὺ δὲ ὀδυνᾶσαι.
²⁶ καὶ ἐν πᾶσι τούτοις μεταξὺ ἡμῶν καὶ ὑμῶν χάσμα μέγα ἐστήρικται,
ὅπως οἱ θέλοντες διαβῆναι ἔνθεν πρὸς ὑμᾶς μὴ δύνωνται, μηδὲ ἐκεῖθεν πρὸς
ἡμᾶς διαπερῶσιν. ²⁷ εἶπεν δέ, Ἐρωτῶ σε οὖν, πάτερ, ἵνα πέμψῃς αὐτὸν εἰς
τὸν οἶκον τοῦ πατρός μου, ²⁸ ἔχω γὰρ πέντε ἀδελφούς, ὅπως διαμαρτύρηται
αὐτοῖς, ἵνα μὴ καὶ αὐτοὶ ἔλθωσιν εἰς τὸν τόπον τοῦτον τῆς βασάνου. ²⁹ λέγει
δὲ Ἀβραάμ, Ἔχουσι Μωϋσέα καὶ τοὺς προφήτας· ἀκουσάτωσαν αὐτῶν. ³⁰
ὁ δὲ εἶπεν, Οὐχί, πάτερ Ἀβραάμ, ἀλλ' ἐάν τις ἀπὸ νεκρῶν πορευθῇ πρὸς
αὐτοὺς μετανοήσουσιν. ³¹ εἶπεν δὲ αὐτῷ, Εἰ Μωϋσέως καὶ τῶν προφητῶν
οὐκ ἀκούουσιν, οὐδ' ἐάν τις ἐκ νεκρῶν ἀναστῇ πεισθήσονται.

English

¹⁹ "There was a rich man who was dressed in purple and fine linen and
who feasted sumptuously every day. ²⁰ And at his gate lay a poor man
named Lazarus, covered with sores, ²¹ who longed to satisfy his hunger
with what fell from the rich man's table; even the dogs would come and
lick his sores. ²² The poor man died and was carried away by the angels
to be with Abraham. The rich man also died and was buried. ²³ In Hades,
where he was being tormented, he looked up and saw Abraham far away
with Lazarus by his side. ²⁴ He called out, 'Father Abraham, have mercy
on me, and send Lazarus to dip the tip of his finger in water and cool my
tongue; for I am in agony in these flames.' ²⁵ But Abraham said, 'Child,
remember that during your lifetime you received your good things, and
Lazarus in like manner evil things; but now he is comforted here, and
you are in agony. ²⁶ Besides all this, between you and us a great chasm
has been fixed, so that those who might want to pass from here to you
cannot do so, and no one can cross from there to us.' ²⁷ He said, 'Then,
father, I beg you to send him to my father's house— ²⁸ for I have five
brothers—that he may warn them, so that they will not also come into
this place of torment.' ²⁹ Abraham replied, 'They have Moses and the
prophets; they should listen to them.' ³⁰ He said, 'No, father Abraham;
but if someone goes to them from the dead, they will repent.' ³¹ He said
to him, 'If they do not listen to Moses and the prophets, neither will they
be convinced even if someone rises from the dead.'"

JESUS CLEANSES TEN LEPERS (17:11–19)

Greek

¹¹ Καὶ ἐγένετο ἐν τῷ πορεύεσθαι εἰς Ἰερουσαλὴμ καὶ αὐτὸς διήρχετο διὰ μέσον Σαμαρείας καὶ Γαλιλαίας. ¹² καὶ εἰσερχομένου αὐτοῦ εἴς τινα κώμην ἀπήντησαν [αὐτῷ] δέκα λεπροὶ ἄνδρες, οἳ ἔστησαν πόρρωθεν, ¹³ καὶ αὐτοὶ ἦραν φωνὴν λέγοντες, Ἰησοῦ ἐπιστάτα, ἐλέησον ἡμᾶς. ¹⁴ καὶ ἰδὼν εἶπεν αὐτοῖς, Πορευθέντες ἐπιδείξατε ἑαυτοὺς τοῖς ἱερεῦσιν. καὶ ἐγένετο ἐν τῷ ὑπάγειν αὐτοὺς ἐκαθαρίσθησαν. ¹⁵ εἷς δὲ ἐξ αὐτῶν, ἰδὼν ὅτι ἰάθη, ὑπέστρεψεν μετὰ φωνῆς μεγάλης δοξάζων τὸν θεόν, ¹⁶ καὶ ἔπεσεν ἐπὶ πρόσωπον παρὰ τοὺς πόδας αὐτοῦ εὐχαριστῶν αὐτῷ· καὶ αὐτὸς ἦν Σαμαρίτης. ¹⁷ ἀποκριθεὶς δὲ ὁ Ἰησοῦς εἶπεν, Οὐχὶ οἱ δέκα ἐκαθαρίσθησαν; οἱ δὲ ἐννέα ποῦ; ¹⁸ οὐχ εὑρέθησαν ὑποστρέψαντες δοῦναι δόξαν τῷ θεῷ εἰ μὴ ὁ ἀλλογενὴς οὗτος; ¹⁹ καὶ εἶπεν αὐτῷ, Ἀναστὰς πορεύου· ἡ πίστις σου σέσωκέν σε.

English

¹¹ On the way to Jerusalem Jesus was going through the region between Samaria and Galilee. ¹² As he entered a village, ten lepers approached him. Keeping their distance, ¹³ they called out, saying, "Jesus, Master, have mercy on us!" ¹⁴ When he saw them, he said to them, "Go and show yourselves to the priests." And as they went, they were made clean. ¹⁵ Then one of them, when he saw that he was healed, turned back, praising God with a loud voice. ¹⁶ He prostrated himself at Jesus' feet and thanked him. And he was a Samaritan. ¹⁷ Then Jesus asked, "Were not ten made clean? But the other nine, where are they? ¹⁸ Was none of them found to return and give praise to God except this foreigner?" ¹⁹ Then he said to him, "Get up and go on your way; your faith has made you well."

PARABLE OF WIDOW AND UNJUST JUDGE (18:1–8)

Greek

¹ Ἔλεγεν δὲ παραβολὴν αὐτοῖς πρὸς τὸ δεῖν πάντοτε προσεύχεσθαι αὐτοὺς καὶ μὴ ἐγκακεῖν, ² λέγων, Κριτής τις ἦν ἔν τινι πόλει τὸν θεὸν μὴ φοβούμενος καὶ ἄνθρωπον μὴ ἐντρεπόμενος. ³ χήρα δὲ ἦν ἐν τῇ πόλει ἐκείνῃ καὶ ἤρχετο πρὸς αὐτὸν λέγουσα, Ἐκδίκησόν με ἀπὸ τοῦ ἀντιδίκου μου.

⁴ καὶ οὐκ ἤθελεν ἐπὶ χρόνον, μετὰ δὲ ταῦτα εἶπεν ἐν ἑαυτῷ, Εἰ καὶ τὸν θεὸν οὐ φοβοῦμαι οὐδὲ ἄνθρωπον ἐντρέπομαι, ⁵ διά γε τὸ παρέχειν μοι κόπον τὴν χήραν ταύτην ἐκδικήσω αὐτήν, ἵνα μὴ εἰς τέλος ἐρχομένη ὑπωπιάζῃ με. ⁶ Εἶπεν δὲ ὁ κύριος, Ἀκούσατε τί ὁ κριτὴς τῆς ἀδικίας λέγει· ⁷ ὁ δὲ θεὸς οὐ μὴ ποιήσῃ τὴν ἐκδίκησιν τῶν ἐκλεκτῶν αὐτοῦ τῶν βοώντων αὐτῷ ἡμέρας καὶ νυκτός, καὶ μακροθυμεῖ ἐπ' αὐτοῖς; ⁸ λέγω ὑμῖν ὅτι ποιήσει τὴν ἐκδίκησιν αὐτῶν ἐν τάχει. πλὴν ὁ υἱὸς τοῦ ἀνθρώπου ἐλθὼν ἆρα εὑρήσει τὴν πίστιν ἐπὶ τῆς γῆς;

English

¹ Then Jesus told them a parable about their need to pray always and not to lose heart. ² He said, "In a certain city there was a judge who neither feared God nor had respect for people. ³ In that city there was a widow who kept coming to him and saying, 'Grant me justice against my opponent.' ⁴ For a while he refused; but later he said to himself, 'Though I have no fear of God and no respect for anyone, ⁵ yet because this widow keeps bothering me, I will grant her justice, so that she may not wear me out by continually coming.'" ⁶ And the Lord said, "Listen to what the unjust judge says. ⁷ And will not God grant justice to his chosen ones who cry to him day and night? Will he delay long in helping them? ⁸ I tell you, he will quickly grant justice to them. And yet, when the Son of Man comes, will he find faith on earth?"

PARABLE OF PHARISEE AND TAX COLLECTOR (18:9–14)

Greek

⁹ Εἶπεν δὲ καὶ πρός τινας τοὺς πεποιθότας ἐφ' ἑαυτοῖς ὅτι εἰσὶν δίκαιοι καὶ ἐξουθενοῦντας τοὺς λοιποὺς τὴν παραβολὴν ταύτην· ¹⁰ Ἄνθρωποι δύο ἀνέβησαν εἰς τὸ ἱερὸν προσεύξασθαι, ὁ εἷς Φαρισαῖος καὶ ὁ ἕτερος τελώνης. ¹¹ ὁ Φαρισαῖος σταθεὶς πρὸς ἑαυτὸν ταῦτα προσηύχετο, Ὁ θεός, εὐχαριστῶ σοι ὅτι οὐκ εἰμὶ ὥσπερ οἱ λοιποὶ τῶν ἀνθρώπων, ἅρπαγες, ἄδικοι, μοιχοί, ἢ καὶ ὡς οὗτος ὁ τελώνης· ¹² νηστεύω δὶς τοῦ σαββάτου, ἀποδεκατῶ πάντα ὅσα κτῶμαι. ¹³ ὁ δὲ τελώνης μακρόθεν ἑστὼς οὐκ ἤθελεν οὐδὲ τοὺς ὀφθαλμοὺς ἐπᾶραι εἰς τὸν οὐρανόν, ἀλλ' ἔτυπτεν τὸ στῆθος αὐτοῦ λέγων, Ὁ θεός, ἱλάσθητί μοι τῷ ἁμαρτωλῷ. ¹⁴ λέγω ὑμῖν, κατέβη οὗτος δεδικαιωμένος εἰς τὸν οἶκον αὐτοῦ παρ' ἐκεῖνον· ὅτι πᾶς ὁ ὑψῶν ἑαυτὸν ταπεινωθήσεται, ὁ δὲ ταπεινῶν ἑαυτὸν ὑψωθήσεται.

English

⁹ He also told this parable to some who trusted in themselves that they were righteous and regarded others with contempt: ¹⁰ "Two men went up to the temple to pray, one a Pharisee and the other a tax collector. ¹¹ The Pharisee, standing by himself, was praying thus, 'God, I thank you that I am not like other people: thieves, rogues, adulterers, or even like this tax collector. ¹² I fast twice a week; I give a tenth of all my income.' ¹³ But the tax collector, standing far off, would not even look up to heaven, but was beating his breast and saying, 'God, be merciful to me, a sinner!' ¹⁴ I tell you, this man went down to his home justified rather than the other; for all who exalt themselves will be humbled, but all who humble themselves will be exalted."

JESUS AND ZACCHAEUS (19:1–10)

Greek

¹ Καὶ εἰσελθὼν διήρχετο τὴν Ἰεριχώ. ² καὶ ἰδοὺ ἀνὴρ ὀνόματι καλούμενος Ζακχαῖος, καὶ αὐτὸς ἦν ἀρχιτελώνης καὶ αὐτὸς πλούσιος. ³ καὶ ἐζήτει ἰδεῖν τὸν Ἰησοῦν τίς ἐστιν, καὶ οὐκ ἠδύνατο ἀπὸ τοῦ ὄχλου ὅτι τῇ ἡλικίᾳ μικρὸς ἦν. ⁴ καὶ προδραμὼν εἰς τὸ ἔμπροσθεν ἀνέβη ἐπὶ συκομορέαν ἵνα ἴδῃ αὐτόν, ὅτι ἐκείνης ἤμελλεν διέρχεσθαι. ⁵ καὶ ὡς ἦλθεν ἐπὶ τὸν τόπον, ἀναβλέψας ὁ Ἰησοῦς εἶπεν πρὸς αὐτόν, Ζακχαῖε, σπεύσας κατάβηθι, σήμερον γὰρ ἐν τῷ οἴκῳ σου δεῖ με μεῖναι. ⁶ καὶ σπεύσας κατέβη, καὶ ὑπεδέξατο αὐτὸν χαίρων. ⁷ καὶ ἰδόντες πάντες διεγόγγυζον λέγοντες ὅτι Παρὰ ἁμαρτωλῷ ἀνδρὶ εἰσῆλθεν καταλῦσαι. ⁸ σταθεὶς δὲ Ζακχαῖος εἶπεν πρὸς τὸν κύριον, Ἰδοὺ τὰ ἡμίσειά μου τῶν ὑπαρχόντων, κύριε, τοῖς πτωχοῖς δίδωμι, καὶ εἴ τινός τι ἐσυκοφάντησα ἀποδίδωμι τετραπλοῦν. ⁹ εἶπεν δὲ πρὸς αὐτὸν ὁ Ἰησοῦς ὅτι Σήμερον σωτηρία τῷ οἴκῳ τούτῳ ἐγένετο, καθότι καὶ αὐτὸς υἱὸς Ἀβραάμ ἐστιν· ¹⁰ ἦλθεν γὰρ ὁ υἱὸς τοῦ ἀνθρώπου ζητῆσαι καὶ σῶσαι τὸ ἀπολωλός.

English

¹ He entered Jericho and was passing through it. ² A man was there named Zacchaeus; he was a chief tax collector and was rich. ³ He was trying to see who Jesus was, but on account of the crowd he could not, because he was short in stature. ⁴ So he ran ahead and climbed a sycamore tree to see him, because he was going to pass that way. ⁵ When Jesus came

to the place, he looked up and said to him, "Zacchaeus, hurry and come down; for I must stay at your house today." 6 So he hurried down and was happy to welcome him. 7 All who saw it began to grumble and said, "He has gone to be the guest of one who is a sinner." 8 Zacchaeus stood there and said to the Lord, "Look, half of my possessions, Lord, I will give to the poor; and if I have defrauded anyone of anything, I will pay back four times as much." 9 Then Jesus said to him, "Today salvation has come to this house, because he too is a son of Abraham. 10 For the Son of Man came to seek out and to save the lost."

JESUS WEEPS OVER JERUSALEM (19:41–44)

Greek

41 Καὶ ὡς ἤγγισεν, ἰδὼν τὴν πόλιν ἔκλαυσεν ἐπ' αὐτήν, 42 λέγων ὅτι Εἰ ἔγνως ἐν τῇ ἡμέρᾳ ταύτῃ καὶ σὺ τὰ πρὸς εἰρήνην – νῦν δὲ ἐκρύβη ἀπὸ ὀφθαλμῶν σου. 43 ὅτι ἥξουσιν ἡμέραι ἐπὶ σὲ καὶ παρεμβαλοῦσιν οἱ ἐχθροί σου χάρακά σοι καὶ περικυκλώσουσίν σε καὶ συνέξουσίν σε πάντοθεν, 44 καὶ ἐδαφιοῦσίν σε καὶ τὰ τέκνα σου ἐν σοί, καὶ οὐκ ἀφήσουσιν λίθον ἐπὶ λίθον ἐν σοί, ἀνθ' ὧν οὐκ ἔγνως τὸν καιρὸν τῆς ἐπισκοπῆς σου.

English

41 As he came near and saw the city, he wept over it, 42 saying, "If you, even you, had only recognized on this day the things that make for peace! But now they are hidden from your eyes. 43 Indeed, the days will come upon you, when your enemies will set up ramparts around you and surround you, and hem you in on every side. 44 They will crush you to the ground, you and your children within you, and they will not leave within you one stone upon another; because you did not recognize the time of your visitation from God."

JESUS' PRAYER FOR PETER (22:31–32)

Greek

31 Σίμων Σίμων, ἰδοὺ ὁ Σατανᾶς ἐξητήσατο ὑμᾶς τοῦ σινιάσαι ὡς τὸν σῖτον· 32 ἐγὼ δὲ ἐδεήθην περὶ σοῦ ἵνα μὴ ἐκλίπῃ ἡ πίστις σου· καὶ σύ ποτε ἐπιστρέψας στήρισον τοὺς ἀδελφούς σου.

English

³¹ "Simon, Simon, listen! Satan has demanded to sift all of you like wheat, ³² but I have prayed for you that your own faith may not fail; and you, when once you have turned back, strengthen your brothers."

PURSE, BAG, AND SWORD (22:35–38)

Greek

³⁵ Καὶ εἶπεν αὐτοῖς, Ὅτε ἀπέστειλα ὑμᾶς ἄτερ βαλλαντίου καὶ πήρας καὶ ὑποδημάτων, μή τινος ὑστερήσατε; οἱ δὲ εἶπαν, Οὐθενός. ³⁶ εἶπεν δὲ αὐτοῖς, Ἀλλὰ νῦν ὁ ἔχων βαλλάντιον ἀράτω, ὁμοίως καὶ πήραν, καὶ ὁ μὴ ἔχων πωλησάτω τὸ ἱμάτιον αὐτοῦ καὶ ἀγορασάτω μάχαιραν. ³⁷ λέγω γὰρ ὑμῖν ὅτι τοῦτο τὸ γεγραμμένον δεῖ τελεσθῆναι ἐν ἐμοί, τὸ Καὶ μετὰ ἀνόμων ἐλογίσθη· καὶ γὰρ τὸ περὶ ἐμοῦ τέλος ἔχει. ³⁸ οἱ δὲ εἶπαν, Κύριε, ἰδοὺ μάχαιραι ὧδε δύο. ὁ δὲ εἶπεν αὐτοῖς, Ἱκανόν ἐστιν.

English

³⁵ He said to them, "When I sent you out without a purse, bag, or sandals, did you lack anything?" They said, "No, not a thing." ³⁶ He said to them, "But now, the one who has a purse must take it, and likewise a bag. And the one who has no sword must sell his cloak and buy one. ³⁷ For I tell you, this scripture must be fulfilled in me, 'And he was counted among the lawless'; and indeed what is written about me is being fulfilled." ³⁸ They said, "Lord, look, here are two swords." He replied, "It is enough."

JESUS BEFORE HEROD (23:6–12)

Greek

⁶ Πιλᾶτος δὲ ἀκούσας ἐπηρώτησεν εἰ ὁ ἄνθρωπος Γαλιλαῖός ἐστιν· ⁷ καὶ ἐπιγνοὺς ὅτι ἐκ τῆς ἐξουσίας Ἡρῴδου ἐστὶν ἀνέπεμψεν αὐτὸν πρὸς Ἡρῴδην, ὄντα καὶ αὐτὸν ἐν Ἱεροσολύμοις ἐν ταύταις ταῖς ἡμέραις. ⁸ ὁ δὲ Ἡρῴδης ἰδὼν τὸν Ἰησοῦν ἐχάρη λίαν, ἦν γὰρ ἐξ ἱκανῶν χρόνων θέλων ἰδεῖν αὐτὸν διὰ τὸ ἀκούειν περὶ αὐτοῦ, καὶ ἤλπιζέν τι σημεῖον ἰδεῖν ὑπ' αὐτοῦ γινόμενον. ⁹ ἐπηρώτα δὲ αὐτὸν ἐν λόγοις ἱκανοῖς· αὐτὸς δὲ οὐδὲν ἀπεκρίνατο αὐτῷ. ¹⁰ εἱστήκεισαν δὲ οἱ ἀρχιερεῖς καὶ οἱ γραμματεῖς εὐτόνως

κατηγοροῦντες αὐτοῦ. ¹¹ ἐξουθενήσας δὲ αὐτὸν [καὶ] ὁ Ἡρῴδης σὺν τοῖς στρατεύμασιν αὐτοῦ καὶ ἐμπαίξας περιβαλὼν ἐσθῆτα λαμπρὰν ἀνέπεμψεν αὐτὸν τῷ Πιλάτῳ. ¹² ἐγένοντο δὲ φίλοι ὅ τε Ἡρῴδης καὶ ὁ Πιλᾶτος ἐν αὐτῇ τῇ ἡμέρᾳ μετ' ἀλλήλων· προϋπῆρχον γὰρ ἐν ἔχθρᾳ ὄντες πρὸς αὐτούς.

English

⁶ When Pilate heard this, he asked whether the man was a Galilean. ⁷ And when he learned that he was under Herod's jurisdiction, he sent him off to Herod, who was himself in Jerusalem at that time. ⁸ When Herod saw Jesus, he was very glad, for he had been wanting to see him for a long time, because he had heard about him and was hoping to see him perform some sign. ⁹ He questioned him at some length, but Jesus gave him no answer. ¹⁰ The chief priests and the scribes stood by, vehemently accusing him. ¹¹ Even Herod with his soldiers treated him with contempt and mocked him; then he put an elegant robe on him, and sent him back to Pilate. ¹² That same day Herod and Pilate became friends with each other; before this they had been enemies.

PILATE DECLARES JESUS INNOCENT (23:13–16)

Greek

¹³ Πιλᾶτος δὲ συγκαλεσάμενος τοὺς ἀρχιερεῖς καὶ τοὺς ἄρχοντας καὶ τὸν λαὸν ¹⁴ εἶπεν πρὸς αὐτούς, Προσηνέγκατέ μοι τὸν ἄνθρωπον τοῦτον ὡς ἀποστρέφοντα τὸν λαόν, καὶ ἰδοὺ ἐγὼ ἐνώπιον ὑμῶν ἀνακρίνας οὐθὲν εὗρον ἐν τῷ ἀνθρώπῳ τούτῳ αἴτιον ὧν κατηγορεῖτε κατ' αὐτοῦ, ¹⁵ ἀλλ' οὐδὲ Ἡρῴδης· ἀνέπεμψεν γὰρ αὐτὸν πρὸς ἡμᾶς· καὶ ἰδοὺ οὐδὲν ἄξιον θανάτου ἐστὶν πεπραγμένον αὐτῷ. ¹⁶ παιδεύσας οὖν αὐτὸν ἀπολύσω.

English

¹³ Pilate then called together the chief priests, the leaders, and the people, ¹⁴ and said to them, "You brought me this man as one who was perverting the people; and here I have examined him in your presence and have not found this man guilty of any of your charges against him. ¹⁵ Neither has Herod, for he sent him back to us. Indeed, he has done nothing to deserve death. ¹⁶ I will therefore have him flogged and release him."

SAYINGS ABOUT JESUS' DEATH (23:28–31, 34, 43, 46)

Greek

²⁸ στραφεὶς δὲ πρὸς αὐτὰς [ὁ] Ἰησοῦς εἶπεν, Θυγατέρες Ἰερουσαλήμ, μὴ κλαίετε ἐπ᾽ ἐμέ· πλὴν ἐφ᾽ ἑαυτὰς κλαίετε καὶ ἐπὶ τὰ τέκνα ὑμῶν, ²⁹ ὅτι ἰδοὺ ἔρχονται ἡμέραι ἐν αἷς ἐροῦσιν, Μακάριαι αἱ στεῖραι καὶ αἱ κοιλίαι αἳ οὐκ ἐγέννησαν καὶ μαστοὶ οἳ οὐκ ἔθρεψαν. ³⁰ τότε ἄρξονται λέγειν τοῖς ὄρεσιν, Πέσετε ἐφ᾽ ἡμᾶς, καὶ τοῖς βουνοῖς, Καλύψατε ἡμᾶς· ³¹ ὅτι εἰ ἐν τῷ ὑγρῷ ξύλῳ ταῦτα ποιοῦσιν, ἐν τῷ ξηρῷ τί γένηται;

³⁴ [ὁ δὲ Ἰησοῦς ἔλεγεν, Πάτερ, ἄφες αὐτοῖς, οὐ γὰρ οἴδασιν τί ποιοῦσιν.] διαμεριζόμενοι δὲ τὰ ἱμάτια αὐτοῦ ἔβαλον κλῆρον.

⁴³ καὶ εἶπεν αὐτῷ, Ἀμήν σοι λέγω, σήμερον μετ᾽ ἐμοῦ ἔσῃ ἐν τῷ παραδείσῳ.

⁴⁶ καὶ φωνήσας φωνῇ μεγάλῃ ὁ Ἰησοῦς εἶπεν, Πάτερ, εἰς χεῖράς σου παρατίθεμαι τὸ πνεῦμά μου· τοῦτο δὲ εἰπὼν ἐξέπνευσεν.

English

²⁸ But Jesus turned to them and said, "Daughters of Jerusalem, do not weep for me, but weep for yourselves and for your children. ²⁹ For the days are surely coming when they will say, 'Blessed are the barren, and the wombs that never bore, and the breasts that never nursed.' ³⁰ Then they will begin to say to the mountains, 'Fall on us'; and to the hills, 'Cover us.' ³¹ For if they do this when the wood is green, what will happen when it is dry?"

³⁴ Then Jesus said, "Father, forgive them; for they do not know what they are doing." And they cast lots to divide his clothing.

⁴³ He replied, "Truly I tell you, today you will be with me in Paradise."

⁴⁶ Then Jesus, crying with a loud voice, said, "Father, into your hands I commend my spirit." Having said this, he breathed his last.

ROAD TO EMMAUS (24:13–35)

Greek

¹³ Καὶ ἰδοὺ δύο ἐξ αὐτῶν ἐν αὐτῇ τῇ ἡμέρᾳ ἦσαν πορευόμενοι εἰς κώμην ἀπέχουσαν σταδίους ἑξήκοντα ἀπὸ Ἰερουσαλήμ, ᾗ ὄνομα Ἐμμαοῦς, ¹⁴ καὶ αὐτοὶ ὡμίλουν πρὸς ἀλλήλους περὶ πάντων τῶν συμβεβηκότων τούτων. ¹⁵ καὶ ἐγένετο ἐν τῷ ὁμιλεῖν αὐτοὺς καὶ συζητεῖν καὶ αὐτὸς Ἰησοῦς ἐγγίσας συνεπορεύετο αὐτοῖς, ¹⁶ οἱ δὲ ὀφθαλμοὶ αὐτῶν ἐκρατοῦντο τοῦ μὴ ἐπιγνῶναι αὐτόν. ¹⁷ εἶπεν δὲ πρὸς αὐτούς, Τίνες οἱ λόγοι οὗτοι οὓς ἀντιβάλλετε πρὸς ἀλλήλους περιπατοῦντες; καὶ ἐστάθησαν σκυθρωποί. ¹⁸ ἀποκριθεὶς δὲ εἷς ὀνόματι Κλεοπᾶς εἶπεν πρὸς αὐτόν, Σὺ μόνος παροικεῖς Ἰερουσαλὴμ καὶ οὐκ ἔγνως τὰ γενόμενα ἐν αὐτῇ ἐν ταῖς ἡμέραις ταύταις; ¹⁹ καὶ εἶπεν αὐτοῖς, Ποῖα; οἱ δὲ εἶπαν αὐτῷ, Τὰ περὶ Ἰησοῦ τοῦ Ναζαρηνοῦ, ὃς ἐγένετο ἀνὴρ προφήτης δυνατὸς ἐν ἔργῳ καὶ λόγῳ ἐναντίον τοῦ θεοῦ καὶ παντὸς τοῦ λαοῦ, ²⁰ ὅπως τε παρέδωκαν αὐτὸν οἱ ἀρχιερεῖς καὶ οἱ ἄρχοντες ἡμῶν εἰς κρίμα θανάτου καὶ ἐσταύρωσαν αὐτόν. ²¹ ἡμεῖς δὲ ἠλπίζομεν ὅτι αὐτός ἐστιν ὁ μέλλων λυτροῦσθαι τὸν Ἰσραήλ· ἀλλά γε καὶ σὺν πᾶσιν τούτοις τρίτην ταύτην ἡμέραν ἄγει ἀφ᾽ οὗ ταῦτα ἐγένετο. ²² ἀλλὰ καὶ γυναῖκές τινες ἐξ ἡμῶν ἐξέστησαν ἡμᾶς· γενόμεναι ὀρθριναὶ ἐπὶ τὸ μνημεῖον ²³ καὶ μὴ εὑροῦσαι τὸ σῶμα αὐτοῦ ἦλθον λέγουσαι καὶ ὀπτασίαν ἀγγέλων ἑωρακέναι, οἳ λέγουσιν αὐτὸν ζῆν. ²⁴ καὶ ἀπῆλθόν τινες τῶν σὺν ἡμῖν ἐπὶ τὸ μνημεῖον, καὶ εὗρον οὕτως καθὼς καὶ αἱ γυναῖκες εἶπον, αὐτὸν δὲ οὐκ εἶδον. ²⁵ καὶ αὐτὸς εἶπεν πρὸς αὐτούς, Ὦ ἀνόητοι καὶ βραδεῖς τῇ καρδίᾳ τοῦ πιστεύειν ἐπὶ πᾶσιν οἷς ἐλάλησαν οἱ προφῆται· ²⁶ οὐχὶ ταῦτα ἔδει παθεῖν τὸν Χριστὸν καὶ εἰσελθεῖν εἰς τὴν δόξαν αὐτοῦ; ²⁷ καὶ ἀρξάμενος ἀπὸ Μωϋσέως καὶ ἀπὸ πάντων τῶν προφητῶν διερμήνευσεν αὐτοῖς ἐν πάσαις ταῖς γραφαῖς τὰ περὶ ἑαυτοῦ. ²⁸ Καὶ ἤγγισαν εἰς τὴν κώμην οὗ ἐπορεύοντο, καὶ αὐτὸς προσεποιήσατο πορρώτερον πορεύεσθαι. ²⁹ καὶ παρεβιάσαντο αὐτὸν λέγοντες, Μεῖνον μεθ᾽ ἡμῶν, ὅτι πρὸς ἑσπέραν ἐστὶν καὶ κέκλικεν ἤδη ἡ ἡμέρα. καὶ εἰσῆλθεν τοῦ μεῖναι σὺν αὐτοῖς. ³⁰ καὶ ἐγένετο ἐν τῷ κατακλιθῆναι αὐτὸν μετ᾽ αὐτῶν λαβὼν τὸν ἄρτον εὐλόγησεν καὶ κλάσας ἐπεδίδου αὐτοῖς· ³¹ αὐτῶν δὲ διηνοίχθησαν οἱ ὀφθαλμοὶ καὶ ἐπέγνωσαν αὐτόν· καὶ αὐτὸς ἄφαντος ἐγένετο ἀπ᾽ αὐτῶν. ³² καὶ εἶπαν πρὸς ἀλλήλους, Οὐχὶ ἡ καρδία ἡμῶν καιομένη ἦν [ἐν ἡμῖν] ὡς ἐλάλει ἡμῖν ἐν τῇ ὁδῷ, ὡς διήνοιγεν ἡμῖν τὰς γραφάς; ³³ καὶ ἀναστάντες αὐτῇ τῇ ὥρᾳ ὑπέστρεψαν εἰς Ἰερουσαλήμ, καὶ εὗρον ἠθροισμένους τοὺς ἕνδεκα καὶ τοὺς σὺν αὐτοῖς,

³⁴ λέγοντας ὅτι ὄντως ἠγέρθη ὁ κύριος καὶ ὤφθη Σίμωνι. ³⁵ καὶ αὐτοὶ ἐξηγοῦντο τὰ ἐν τῇ ὁδῷ καὶ ὡς ἐγνώσθη αὐτοῖς ἐν τῇ κλάσει τοῦ ἄρτου.

English

¹³ Now on that same day two of them were going to a village called Emmaus, about seven miles from Jerusalem, ¹⁴ and talking with each other about all these things that had happened. ¹⁵ While they were talking and discussing, Jesus himself came near and went with them, ¹⁶ but their eyes were kept from recognizing him. ¹⁷ And he said to them, "What are you discussing with each other while you walk along?" They stood still, looking sad. ¹⁸ Then one of them, whose name was Cleopas, answered him, "Are you the only stranger in Jerusalem who does not know the things that have taken place there in these days?" ¹⁹ He asked them, "What things?" They replied, "The things about Jesus of Nazareth, who was a prophet mighty in deed and word before God and all the people, ²⁰ and how our chief priests and leaders handed him over to be condemned to death and crucified him. ²¹ But we had hoped that he was the one to redeem Israel. Yes, and besides all this, it is now the third day since these things took place. ²² Moreover, some women of our group astounded us. They were at the tomb early this morning, ²³ and when they did not find his body there, they came back and told us that they had indeed seen a vision of angels who said that he was alive. ²⁴ Some of those who were with us went to the tomb and found it just as the women had said; but they did not see him." ²⁵ Then he said to them, "Oh, how foolish you are, and how slow of heart to believe all that the prophets have declared! ²⁶ Was it not necessary that the Messiah should suffer these things and then enter into his glory?" ²⁷ Then beginning with Moses and all the prophets, he interpreted to them the things about himself in all the scriptures. ²⁸ As they came near the village to which they were going, he walked ahead as if he were going on. ²⁹ But they urged him strongly, saying, "Stay with us, because it is almost evening and the day is now nearly over." So he went in to stay with them. ³⁰ When he was at the table with them, he took bread, blessed and broke it, and gave it to them. ³¹ Then their eyes were opened, and they recognized him; and he vanished from their sight. ³² They said to each other, "Were not our hearts burning within us while he was talking to us on the road, while he was opening the scriptures to us?" ³³ That same hour they got up and returned to Jerusalem; and they found the eleven and their companions

gathered together. ³⁴ They were saying, "The Lord has risen indeed, and he has appeared to Simon!" ³⁵ Then they told what had happened on the road, and how he had been made known to them in the breaking of the bread.

APPEARANCE TO THE DISCIPLES (24:36–49)

Greek

³⁶ Ταῦτα δὲ αὐτῶν λαλούντων αὐτὸς ἔστη ἐν μέσῳ αὐτῶν καὶ λέγει αὐτοῖς, Εἰρήνη ὑμῖν. ³⁷ πτοηθέντες δὲ καὶ ἔμφοβοι γενόμενοι ἐδόκουν πνεῦμα θεωρεῖν. ³⁸ καὶ εἶπεν αὐτοῖς, Τί τεταραγμένοι ἐστέ, καὶ διὰ τί διαλογισμοὶ ἀναβαίνουσιν ἐν τῇ καρδίᾳ ὑμῶν; ³⁹ ἴδετε τὰς χεῖράς μου καὶ τοὺς πόδας μου ὅτι ἐγώ εἰμι αὐτός· ψηλαφήσατέ με καὶ ἴδετε, ὅτι πνεῦμα σάρκα καὶ ὀστέα οὐκ ἔχει καθὼς ἐμὲ θεωρεῖτε ἔχοντα. ⁴⁰ καὶ τοῦτο εἰπὼν ἔδειξεν αὐτοῖς τὰς χεῖρας καὶ τοὺς πόδας. ⁴¹ ἔτι δὲ ἀπιστούντων αὐτῶν ἀπὸ τῆς χαρᾶς καὶ θαυμαζόντων εἶπεν αὐτοῖς, Ἔχετέ τι βρώσιμον ἐνθάδε; ⁴² οἱ δὲ ἐπέδωκαν αὐτῷ ἰχθύος ὀπτοῦ μέρος· ⁴³ καὶ λαβὼν ἐνώπιον αὐτῶν ἔφαγεν. ⁴⁴ Εἶπεν δὲ πρὸς αὐτούς, Οὗτοι οἱ λόγοι μου οὓς ἐλάλησα πρὸς ὑμᾶς ἔτι ὢν σὺν ὑμῖν, ὅτι δεῖ πληρωθῆναι πάντα τὰ γεγραμμένα ἐν τῷ νόμῳ Μωϋσέως καὶ τοῖς προφήταις καὶ ψαλμοῖς περὶ ἐμοῦ. ⁴⁵ τότε διήνοιξεν αὐτῶν τὸν νοῦν τοῦ συνιέναι τὰς γραφάς. ⁴⁶ καὶ εἶπεν αὐτοῖς ὅτι Οὕτως γέγραπται παθεῖν τὸν Χριστὸν καὶ ἀναστῆναι ἐκ νεκρῶν τῇ τρίτῃ ἡμέρᾳ, ⁴⁷ καὶ κηρυχθῆναι ἐπὶ τῷ ὀνόματι αὐτοῦ μετάνοιαν καὶ ἄφεσιν ἁμαρτιῶν εἰς πάντα τὰ ἔθνη – ἀρξάμενοι ἀπὸ Ἰερουσαλήμ· ⁴⁸ ὑμεῖς μάρτυρες τούτων. ⁴⁹ καὶ [ἰδοὺ] ἐγὼ ἀποστέλλω τὴν ἐπαγγελίαν τοῦ πατρός μου ἐφ᾽ ὑμᾶς· ὑμεῖς δὲ καθίσατε ἐν τῇ πόλει ἕως οὗ ἐνδύσησθε ἐξ ὕψους δύναμιν.

English

³⁶ While they were talking about this, Jesus himself stood among them and said to them, "Peace be with you." ³⁷ They were startled and terrified, and thought that they were seeing a ghost. ³⁸ He said to them, "Why are you frightened, and why do doubts arise in your hearts? ³⁹ Look at my hands and my feet; see that it is I myself. Touch me and see; for a ghost does not have flesh and bones as you see that I have." ⁴⁰ And when he had said this, he showed them his hands and his feet. ⁴¹ While in their joy they were disbelieving and still wondering, he said to them, "Have you anything here to eat?" ⁴² They gave him a piece of broiled fish, ⁴³ and

he took it and ate in their presence. [44] Then he said to them, "These are my words that I spoke to you while I was still with you—that everything written about me in the law of Moses, the prophets, and the psalms must be fulfilled." [45] Then he opened their minds to understand the scriptures, [46] and he said to them, "Thus it is written, that the Messiah is to suffer and to rise from the dead on the third day, [47] and that repentance and forgiveness of sins is to be proclaimed in his name to all nations, beginning from Jerusalem. [48] You are witnesses of these things. [49] And see, I am sending upon you what my Father promised; so stay here in the city until you have been clothed with power from on high."

JESUS' ASCENSION (24:50–53)

Greek

[50] Ἐξήγαγεν δὲ αὐτοὺς [ἔξω] ἕως πρὸς Βηθανίαν, καὶ ἐπάρας τὰς χεῖρας αὐτοῦ εὐλόγησεν αὐτούς. [51] καὶ ἐγένετο ἐν τῷ εὐλογεῖν αὐτὸν αὐτοὺς διέστη ἀπ᾽ αὐτῶν καὶ ἀνεφέρετο εἰς τὸν οὐρανόν. [52] καὶ αὐτοὶ προσκυνήσαντες αὐτὸν ὑπέστρεψαν εἰς Ἰερουσαλὴμ μετὰ χαρᾶς μεγάλης, [53] καὶ ἦσαν διὰ παντὸς ἐν τῷ ἱερῷ εὐλογοῦντες τὸν θεόν.

English

[50] Then he led them out as far as Bethany, and, lifting up his hands, he blessed them. [51] While he was blessing them, he withdrew from them and was carried up into heaven. [52] And they worshiped him, and returned to Jerusalem with great joy; [53] and they were continually in the temple blessing God.

Appendix

Paffenroth's Reconstruction of L

THE FOLLOWING LIST OF material is based on the reconstruction of L in Paffenroth, *The Story of Jesus according to L*, 159–65. The list that follows was distilled from Paffenroth by Robert E. Van Voorst (*Jesus Outside the New Testament*, 140–41).

Preaching of John the Baptist	3:10–14
Elijah's Miracles for Gentiles	4:25–27
Jesus Raises Son of Widow in Nain	7:11b–15
A Sinful Woman Forgiven	7:36–47
Parable of the Good Samaritan	10:30–37a
Mary and Martha dispute; Mary in the right	10:39–42
Parable of the Persistent Friend	11:5b–8
Parable of the Rich Fool	12:16b–20
Parable of the Doorkeeper	12:35–38
Repent or Perish	13:1b–5
Parable of the Barren Fig Tree	13:6b–9
Healing on the Sabbath	13:10–17b
Warning about Herod, Challenging Response	13:31b–32
Healing on the Sabbath	14:2–5
Parable of Choice of Place at Table	14:8–10, 12–14
Counting the Cost	14:28–32
Parable of the Lost Sheep	15:4–6
Parable of the Lost Coin	15:8–9
Parable of the Lost ("Prodigal") Son	15:11–32
Parable of the Dishonest Manager	16:1b–8

Bibliography

Aland, Kurt, editor. *Synopsis Quattuor Evangeliorum: Locis parallelis evangeliorum apocryphorum et partum adhibit.* 15th rev. ed. Stuttgart: Deutsche Bibelgesellschaft, 1996; 2nd corr. printing, 1997.

Barr, Allan. *A Diagram of Synoptic Relationships (In Four Colours).* Edinburgh: T. & T. Clark: Edinburgh, 1938.

Bauckham, Richard, editor. *The Gospels for All Christians: Rethinking the Gospel Audiences.* Grand Rapids: Eerdmans, 1998.

———. *Jesus and the Eyewitnesses: The Gospels as Eyewitness Testimony.* Grand Rapids: Eerdmans, 2006.

Bellinzoni, Arthur J. Jr., et al., editors. *The Two-Source Hypothesis: A Critical Appraisal.* Macon: Mercer University Press, 1985.

Black, David Alan, and David R. Beck, editors. *Rethinking the Synoptic Problem.* Grand Rapids: Baker, 2001.

Borg, Marcus J, editor. *The Lost Gospel Q: The Original Sayings of Jesus.* Berkeley: Ulysses, 1999.

Boring, Eugene M. "The 'Minor Agreements' and Their Bearing on the Synoptic Problem." In *New Studies in the Synoptic Problem: Oxford Conference, April 2008: Essays in Honour of Christopher M. Tuckett,* edited by Paul Foster et al., 227–251. BETL 239. Leuven: Peeters, 2011.

Brooks, Stephenson H. *Matthew's Community: The Evidence of His Special Sayings Material.* JSNTSup 16. Sheffield: Sheffield Academic Press, 1987.

Brown, Raymond E. *The Birth of the Messiah: A Commentary on the Infancy Narratives in Matthew and Luke.* ABD. Rev. ed. New York: Doubleday, 1993.

Bultmann, Rudolf. *The History of the Synoptic Tradition.* Translated by J. Marsh. New York: Harper & Row, 1963; German original 1921.

Burnett, Fred W. "'M' Tradition." In *Dictionary of Jesus and the Gospels,* edited by Joel B. Green et al., 511–512. Downers Grove: InterVarsity, 1992.

Burton, E. D. W. *Principles of Literary Criticism and the Synoptic Problem.* Chicago: University of Chicago Press, 1904.

Butler, B. C. *The Originality of St. Matthew: A Critique of the Two-Document Hypothesis.* Cambridge: Cambridge University Press, 1951.

Creed, J. M. "'L' and the Structure of the Lucan Gospel: A Study of the Proto-Luke Hypothesis." *ExpTim* 46 (1934–35) 101–07.

Crook, Zeba Antonin. "The Synoptic Parables of the Mustard Seed and the Leaven: A Test-Case for the Two-Document, Two-Gospel, and Farrer-Goulder Hypotheses." *JSNT* 78 (2000) 23–48.

Dawes, Gregory W., editor. *The Historical Jesus Quest: Landmarks in the Search for the Jesus of History.* Louisville: Westminster John Knox, 1999.

Dibelius, Franz. "Die Herkunft der Sonderstücke des Lukas-evangeliums." *ZNW* 12 (1911) 325–43.

Downing, F. G. "Compositional Conventions and the Synoptic Problem." *JBL* 107 (1988) 69–85.

Dungan, David L. *A History of the Synoptic Problem: The Canon, the Text, the Composition, and the Interpretation of the Gospels.* ABD. New York: Doubleday, 1999.

Farmer, William Reuben, editor. *New Synoptic Studies: The Cambridge Gospel Conference and Beyond.* Macon: Mercer University Press, 1983.

——. *The Synoptic Problem: A Critical Analysis.* Dillsboro: Western North Carolina Press, 1976.

Farrer, Austin M. "On Dispensing with Q." In *Studies in the Gospels: Essays in Memory of R. H. Lightfoot,* edited by D. E. Nineham, 57–88. Oxford: Blackwell, 1957.

Fleddermann, Harry T. *Q: A Reconstruction and Commentary.* BiTS 1. Leuven: Peeters, 2005.

Foster, Paul. "The M-Source: Its History and Demise in Biblical Scholarship." In *New Studies in the Synoptic Problem: Oxford Conference, April 2008: Essays in Honour of Christopher M. Tuckett,* edited by Paul Foster et al., 591–616. BETL 239. Leuven: Peeters, 2011.

——, et al., editors. *New Studies in the Synoptic Problem: Oxford Conference, April 2008: Essays in Honour of Christopher M. Tuckett.* BETL 239. Leuven: Peeters, 2011.

Gilmour, S. MacLean. "A Critical Re-examination of Proto-Luke." *JBL* 67 (1948) 378–79.

Goodacre, Mark. *The Synoptic Problem: A Way Through the Maze.* London: Sheffield, 2001.

Goulder, Michael D. "Is Q a Juggernaut?" *JBL* 115 (1996) 667–81.

Griesbach, J. J. *Commentatio qua Marci Evangelium totum e Matthaei et Lucae Commentariis Decerptum esse monstratur* (A Demonstration that Mark Was Written After Matthew and Luke) (Jena, 1789–90). In *J. J. Griesbach: Synoptic and Text-Critical Studies, 1776–1976,* edited by Bernard Orchard, and Thomas R. W. Longstaff, 103–35. SNTSMS 34. Cambridge: Cambridge University Press, 1978.

——. *Synopsis Evangeliorum Matthaei, Marci, et Lucae.* Halle, 1776.

Hawkins, John C. *Horae Synopticae. Contributions to the Study of the Synoptic Problem.* 2nd rev. ed. Oxford: Clarendon, 1909.

Head, Peter M. *Christology and the Synoptic Problem: An Argument for Markan Priority.* SNTSMS 94. Cambridge: Cambridge University Press, 1997.

Henaut, Barry W. *Oral Tradition and the Gospels: The Problem of Mark 4.* JSNTSup 82. Sheffield: JSOT Press, 1993.

Hengel, Martin. *The Four Gospels and the One Gospel of Jesus Christ: An Investigation of the Collection and Origin of the Canonical Gospels.* Harrisburg: Trinity International, 2000.

Kelber, Werner. *The Oral and Written Gospel: The Hermeneutics of Speaking and Writing the Synoptic Tradition, Mark, Paul and Q.* Philadelphia: Fortress, 1983.

Kilpatrick, G. D. *The Origins of the Gospel according to St. Matthew.* Oxford: Clarendon, 1946.

Kloppenborg, John S. *Excavating Q: The History and Setting of the Sayings Gospel.* Minneapolis: Fortress; Edinburgh: T. & T. Clark, 2000.

——. *The Formation of Q: Trajectories in Ancient Wisdom Collections.* Studies in Antiquity and Christianity. Philadelphia: Fortress, 1987.

———, editor. *The Shape of Q: Signal Essays on the Sayings Gospel*. Minneapolis: Fortress, 1994.

———. *Q, The Earliest Gospel: An Introduction to the Original Stories and Sayings of Jesus*. Louisville: Westminster John Knox, 2008.

Knox, W. L. *The Sources of the Synoptic Gospels*. Vol. 2. *St. Luke and St. Matthew*. Cambridge: Cambridge University Press, 1957.

Koester, Helmut. *Ancients Christian Gospels: Their History and Development*. London: SCM; Valley Forge: Trinity Press International, 1990.

———. "Q and Its Relatives." In *Gospel Origins and Christian Beginnings: In Honor of James M. Robinson*, edited by James E. Goehring, Jack T. Sanders, and Charles W. Hedrick, in collaboration with Hans Dieter Betz, 49–63. Sonoma: Polebridge, 1990.

Kümmel, Werner G. *Introduction to the New Testament*. Rev. ed. Translated by Howard Clark Kee. Nashville: Abingdon, 1975.

Longstaff, Thomas R. W., and Page A. Thomas, editors. *The Synoptic Problem: A Bibliography, 1716-1988*. NGS 4. Macon: Mercer University Press, 1988.

Montefiore, H. W. "Does 'L' Hold Water?" *JTS* 12 (1961) 59–60.

Neirynck, Frans. "Goulder and the Minor Agreements." *ETL* 73 (1997) 84–93.

———. *Q-Parallels: Q-Synopsis and IQP/CritEd Parallels*. SNTA 20. Leuven: Peeters, 2001.

Nickle, Keith F. *The Synoptic Gospels: An Introduction*. Atlanta: John Knox, 1980.

Owen, Henry. *Observations on the Four Gospels; Tending Chiefly to Ascertain the Times of Their Publication, and to Illustrate the Form and Manner of Their Composition*. London: T. Payne, 1764.

Paffenroth, Kim. *The Story of Jesus according to L*. JSNTSup 147. Sheffield: Sheffield Academic Press, 1997.

Parrott, D. M. "The Dishonest Steward (Luke 16:1–8a) and Luke's Special Parable Collection." *NTS* 37 (1991) 499–515.

Perrin, Norman. *Rediscovering the Teaching of Jesus*. New York: Harper & Row, 1967.

Powell, Mark Allan. *Fortress Introduction to the Gospels*. Minneapolis: Fortress, 1998.

Robsinson, James M. et al., editors. *The Critical Edition of Q: Synopsis Including the Gospels of Matthew and Luke, Mark and Thomas*. With English, German, and French Translations of Q and Thomas. Philadelphia: Fortress; Leuven: Peeters, 2000.

Sanday, William, editor. *Oxford Studies in the Synoptic Problem: By Members of the University of Oxford*. Oxford: Clarendon, 1911.

Sanders, E. P. *The Tendencies of the Synoptic Tradition*. SNTSMS 9. Cambridge: Cambridge University Press, 1969.

Sanders, E. P., and Margaret Davies. *Studying the Synoptic Gospels*. London: SCM; Valley Forge: Trinity Press International, 1989.

Schnelle, Udo. *The History and Theology of the New Testament Writings*. Minneapolis: Fortress, 1994.

Soards, M. L. *The Passion according to Luke: The Special Material of Luke 22*. JSNTSup 14. Sheffield: Sheffield Academic Press, 1987.

Stein, Robert H. *Studying the Synoptic Gospels: Origin and Interpretation*. 2nd ed. Grand Rapids: Baker, 2001.

———. *The Synoptic Problem: An Introduction*. Grand Rapids: Baker, 1987.

Strauss, David Friedrich. *The Life of Jesus*. Translated by George Eliot. 2 vols. London: Chapman Bro., 1846.

Streeter, B. H. *The Four Gospels: A Study of Origins Treating of the Manuscript Tradition, Sources, Authorship, and Dates*. New York: Macmillan, 1925.

———. "The Literary Evolution of the Gospels." In *Oxford Studies in the Synoptic Problem*, edited by William Sanday, 209–27. Oxford: Clarendon, 1911.

Talbert, Charles H., and Edgar V. McKnight. "Can the Griesbach Hypothesis Be Falsified?" *JBL* 91 (1972) 338–68.

Taylor, Vincent. *Behind the Third Gospel: A Study of the Proto-Luke Hypothesis*. Oxford: Oxford University Press, 1926.

Tuckett, Christopher M. *Q and the History of Early Christianity: Studies on Q*. Edinburgh: T. & T. Clark, 1996.

Voorst, Robert E. Van. *Jesus Outside the Gospels: An Introduction to the Ancient Evidence*. Grand Rapids: Eerdmans, 2000.

Williams, Matthew C. "The OWEN Hypothesis: An Essay Showing That It Was Henry Owen Who First Formulated the So-Called 'Griesbach Hypothesis.'" *JHC* 7 (2000) 126–58.

———. *Two Gospels from One: A Comprehensive Text-Critical Analysis of the Synoptic Gospels*. Grand Rapids: Kregel, 2006.

Wink, Walter. *John the Baptist in the Gospel Tradition*. SNTSMS 7. Cambridge: Cambridge University Press, 1968.

Lightning Source UK Ltd.
Milton Keynes UK
UKOW06f1819220116

266929UK00001BA/216/P